The Massive Book of Guitar Exercises
Over 1800 guitar exercises for every skill level and style!

MW00885999

This book is aimed at guitarists of all levels and styles, as well as bassists. **This book contains more than 1800 exercises!** The exercises cover a wide range of playing skills, techniques, and finger combinations. Without the use of scales or music theory, this is strictly an exercise book that will greatly improve finger speed, strength, picking, and playing techniques. Although no scales are used in this book, the finger combinations and patterns do appear in all scales, solos, riffs, and bass lines.

The exercises are written in tablature (tab). However, because the fingerings are the same as the fret numbers, many of the exercises are shown from the first fret. This makes the exercises much easier to learn, so they can be moved to any other fret. The majority of the exercises include alternate picking and economy picking with fingering suggestions. The exercises are then repeated with hammer-ons and pull-offs. Some guitarists rarely use economy picking and instead prefer alternate picking, hammer-ons, and pull-offs. Economy picking is included because many guitarists use it for speed. It is recommended to work on alternate picking before economy picking.

There are several ways to approach this book: you could practice an entire section over a week, a single exercise per day, or if you are an experienced player, you may want to go directly to exercises that help with a specific technique you want to improve. If some exercises or techniques are too difficult to begin with, switch to another exercise or section and return later.

Consider this book to be a guitar gym. Similar to going to the gym, you would return and repeat the same exercises or focus on a specific area you want to improve. The majority of the exercises in this book are simple to learn and can be played while doing something else, such as watching a movie or listening to music!

When practicing, make sure you're sitting or standing in the correct position for your style or type of guitar. Sit up straight on a chair without arms, not too high (legs should be about 90 degrees), with something under your foot to raise the leg on which the guitar rests to prevent the guitar from sliding down your leg. When standing, adjust your strap so that your fretting hand arm is at about a 45-degree angle.

A metronome is useful, but it can be difficult to use in some situations. Some guitar exercises had to be arranged in unusual time signatures due to their nature and to make them easy to read. One click per note will keep you even and controlled during exercises with unusual time signatures.

Thank you for your support!
For more books and materials, check out:
www.allaboutguitarbooks.com

© 2023 CHRIS L. CONNORS ALL RIGHTS RESERVED

Contents

- *Proper Technique 5*
- *Two Fingers 6*
- *Two Fingers - Switched Up 10*
- *Two Fingers - Three Grouping 12*
- *Three Fingers 15*
- *Three Fingers - Three Grouping 21*
- *Three Fingers - Four Grouping 23*
- *Four Fingers 25*
- *Alternate Picking 31*
- *Economy Picking 32*
- *Four Fingers - Three Grouping 33*
- *Four Fingers - Four Grouping 34*
- *Two and Three Fingers 35*
- *Two and Four Fingers 48*
- *Three and Four Fingers 74*
- *Between Two Strings 86*
- *Between Two Strings 2 93*
- *Turning Around 96*
- *Extended Fingering 106*
- *Linear Exercises 110*
- *Pivoting 1 117*
- *Pivoting 2 122*
- *Return Fingering 127*
- *Sliding Hammer-ons and Pull-offs 130*
- *Spider Walks 133*
- *Spider Walks 2 138*
- *Spider Walks 3 141*
- *String Skipping 144*
- *Sweeping 152*
- *Tapping 155*
- *Two Handed Tapping 161*

Proper Technique

Grip the pick with your thumb and index finger, the point of the pick facing the strings. Grip the pick with just enough force to keep it from falling out of your hand. Depending on what you are playing, the angle at which you hold your pick will vary slightly.

When picking, the pick does not have to be flat against the string; a slight angle of about 45° is normal and will help you reach faster speeds because the angled pick slides past the string with less resistance. A flat picking technique yields very clear, snappy notes.

Experiment with angles ranging from flat to 45 degrees. Most players find a comfortable spot somewhere in the middle.

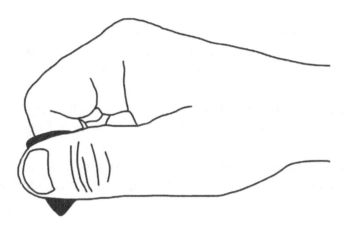

Unless otherwise specified, the fret hand fingers should be on their tips, with the thumb behind the neck and the *thumb print* part of your thumb against the neck pointing upward like a *thumbs-up* gesture. The neck of the guitar should not be cradled in your palm. As you move your hand to different frets, slide your thumb along the back of the neck without dragging it.

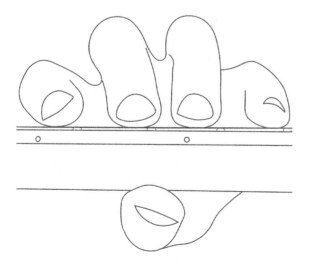

⇨ Tip: Playing on the tips of your fingers does not require you to place each finger precisely on the tip. Follow the natural curve of your fingers as you curl your fingers. You'll notice that not every finger, particularly the first and fourth, stands directly on its tip.

Two Fingers

All combinations of fingers in pairs. This is a great place to start for anyone at any level because these first exercises are easy to play and understand.

The numbers for these first exercises, and most exercises in this book, represent the fingers, not the frets. Exercises should be played on many different frets.

Besides helping with technique and speed, these exercises will help strengthen all possible pairs of fingers and prepare you for the rest of the exercises in this book.

For more advanced players, these exercises will greatly increase your speed and accuracy for playing lines that include two notes per string and will also help with playing pentatonic scales and pentatonic-like riffs or solos faster and smoother.

The exercises are presented first with alternate picking and then again with hammer-ons and pull-offs, followed by alternative patterns for all of the pairs of fingers.

Alternate picking or economy picking can be reversed, producing four ways to play each example: down-up, up-down, down-down, or up-up. Start with alternate picking because this is the most beneficial.

More about economy picking coming up.

⇨ *Tip: If you are a jazz or blues player, try 'swinging your eighths' for any of the exercises in this book.*

Try reversing the picking: up - down.

Alternate picking shown below, economy picking shown above. Start with alternate picking. The H's stand for hammer-on and the P's are pull-offs.

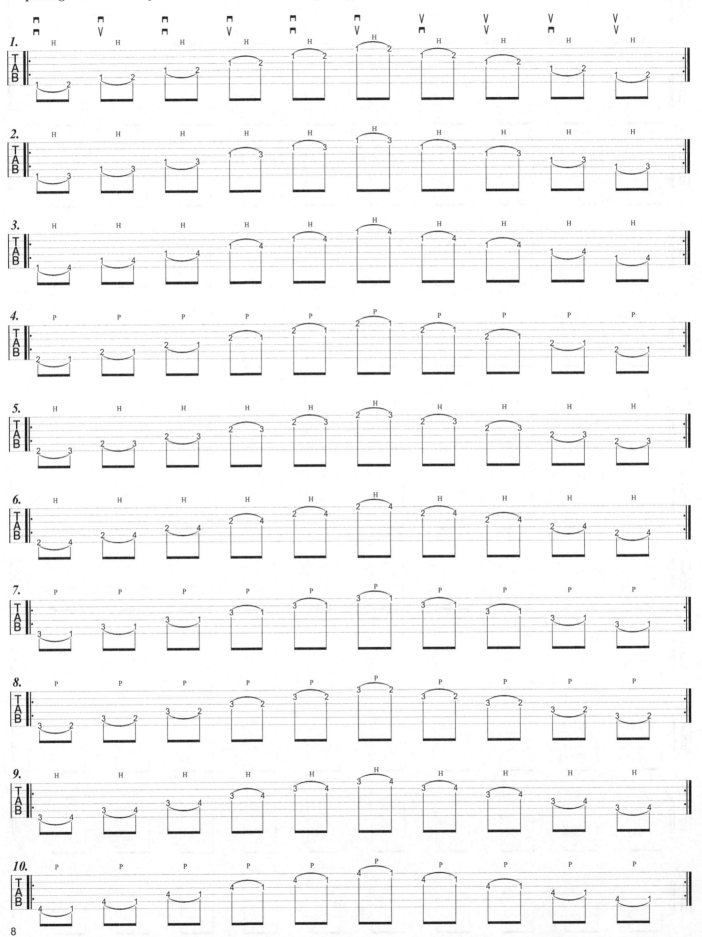

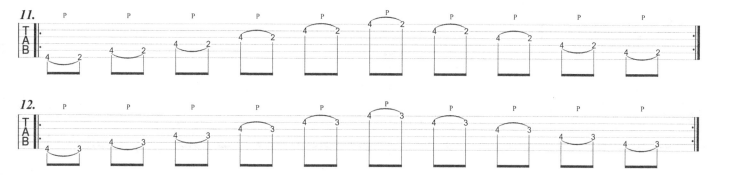

Eight Ways to Play Exercises

Most of the exercises in this book can be played not only from any fret but also in any direction on the fretboard. There are eight directions you can play in!

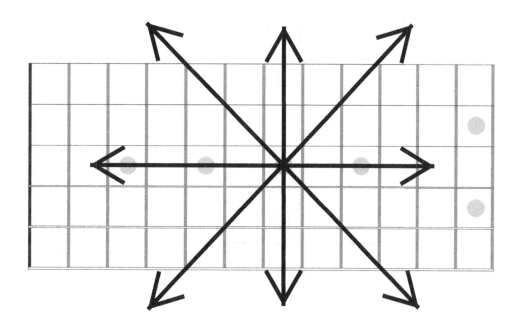

Two Fingers - Switched Up

Ascending and descending should be treated as separate exercises.

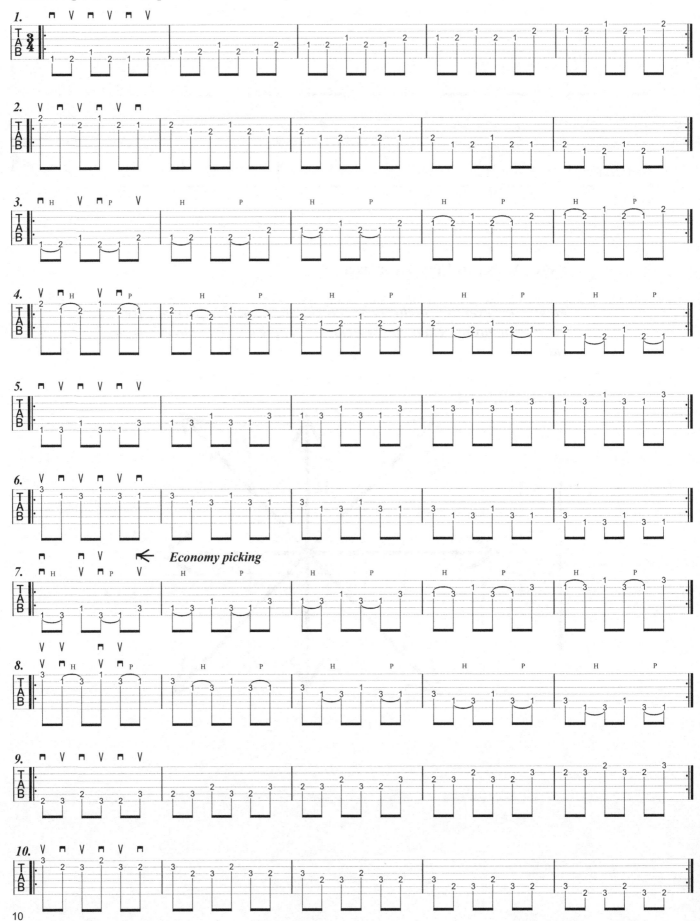

Remember the numbers represent the fingerings, not the frets. Make sure to practice from many different frets.

11.

12.

13.

14.

15.

16.

17.

18.

19.

20.

Two Fingers - Three Grouping

Tip: Three grouping is: up 3 notes, back one note and then up three notes again.

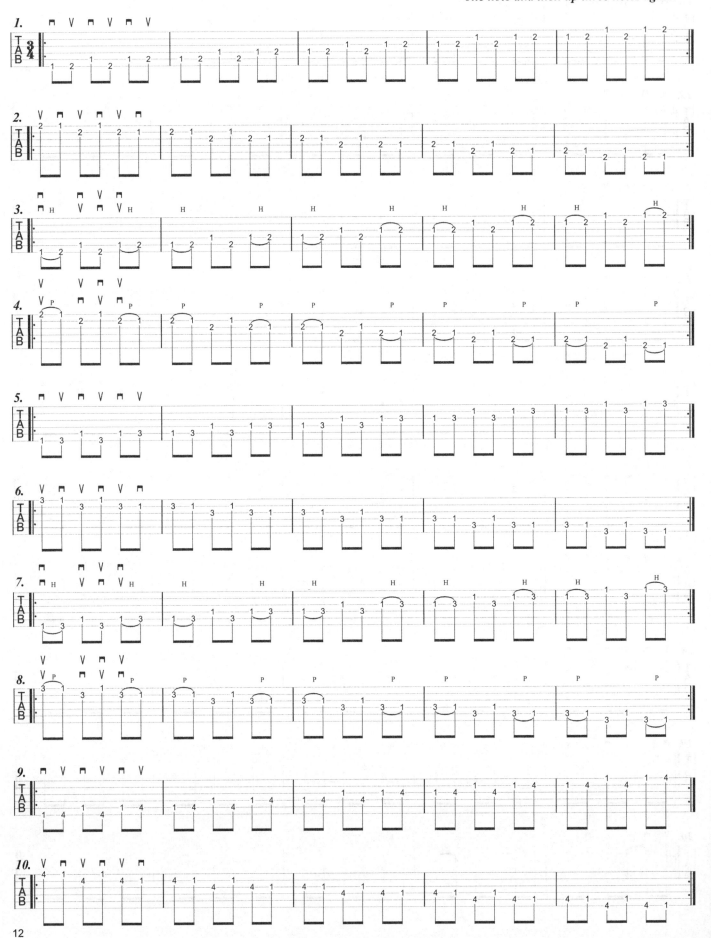

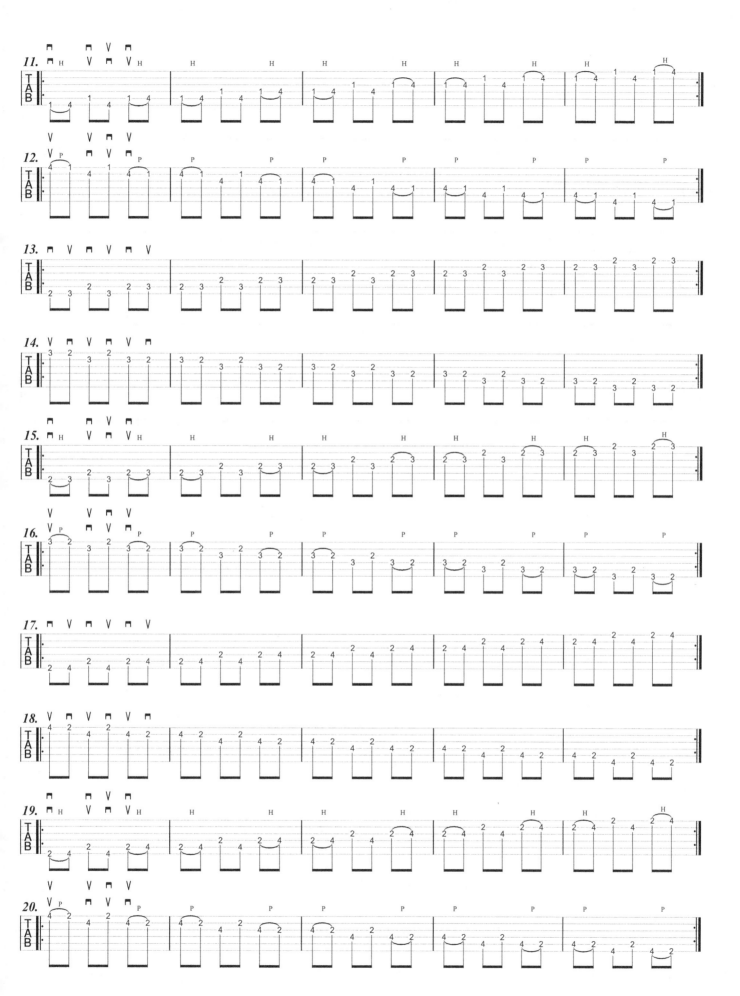

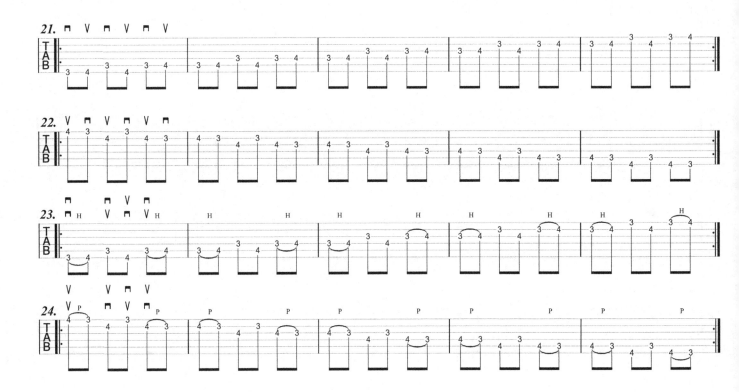

Three Fingers

When playing three notes per string, alternate picking is the best method for purposes of accuracy and being able to switch up rhythms. For some guitarists, economy picking can be beneficial for gaining speed. Alternate picking should be your first method, augmented with economy picking.

Many guitar scales have 3 notes per string within them, and melodies and solos are derived from these scales. These three finger patterns will help you move through scales in new ways, creating patterns that can easily be applied to scales you may already know.

Alternate Picking

Economy Picking

Alternate Picking with Hammer-ons and Pull-offs

Economy Picking with Hammer-ons and Pull-offs

More detail on alternate and economy picking in the upcoming sections.

Tip: The picking can be reversed for all exercises. This simply means that you should begin with up instead of down, and vice versa.

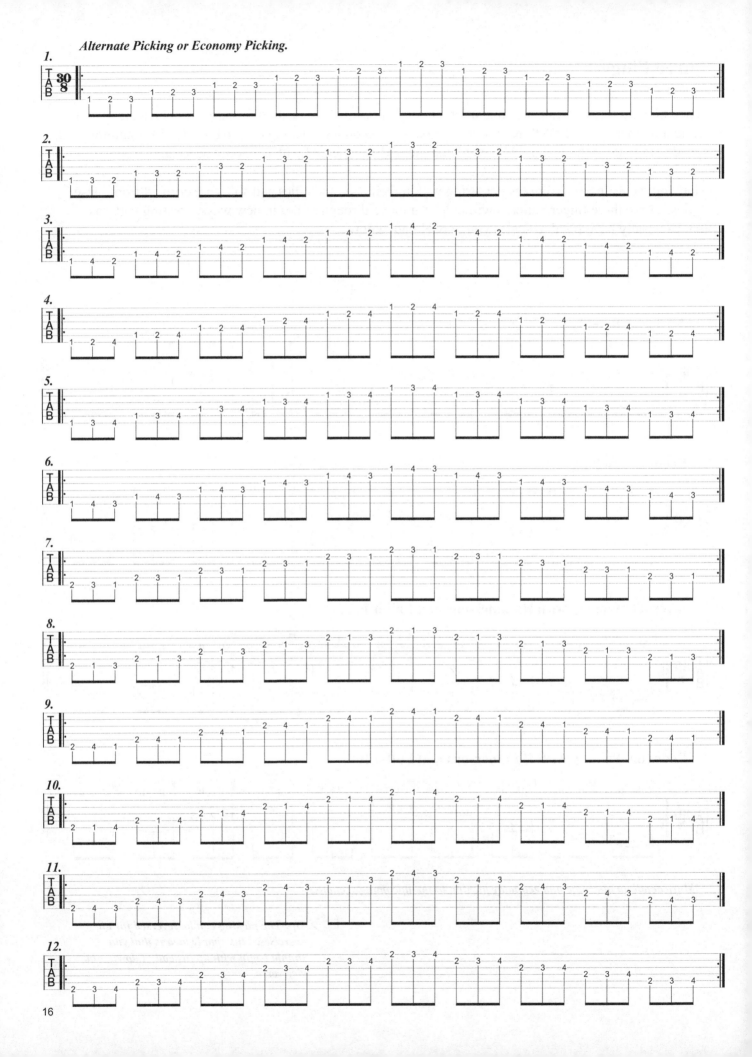

Alternate Picking or Economy Picking.

16

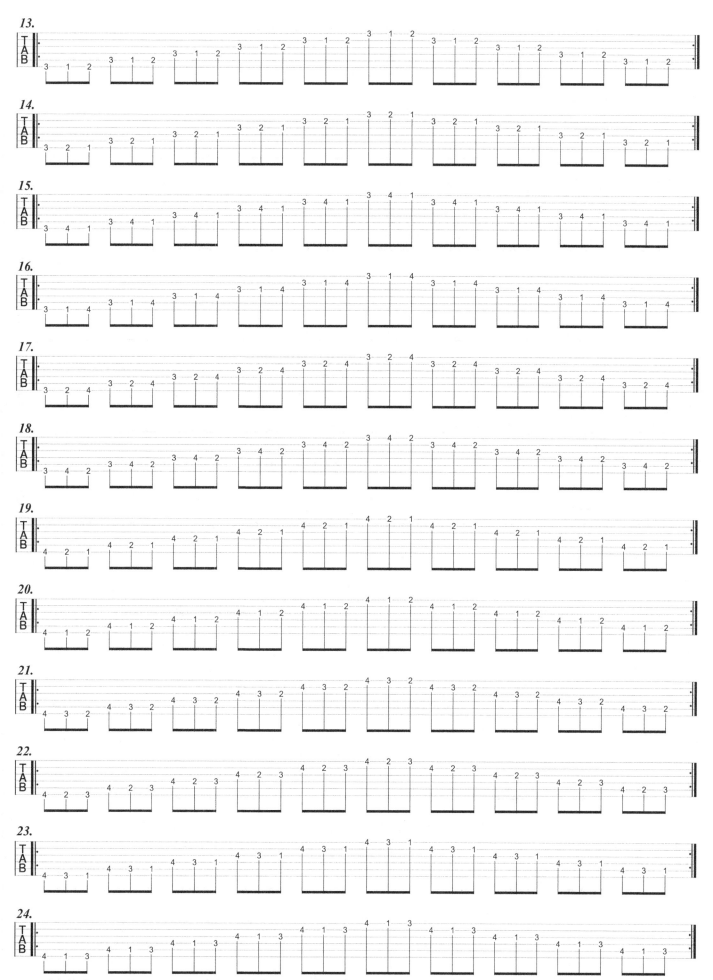

*These exercises are especially useful for building speed and strength.

Pick the first note per every group of three notes using Alternate Picking or Economy Picking.

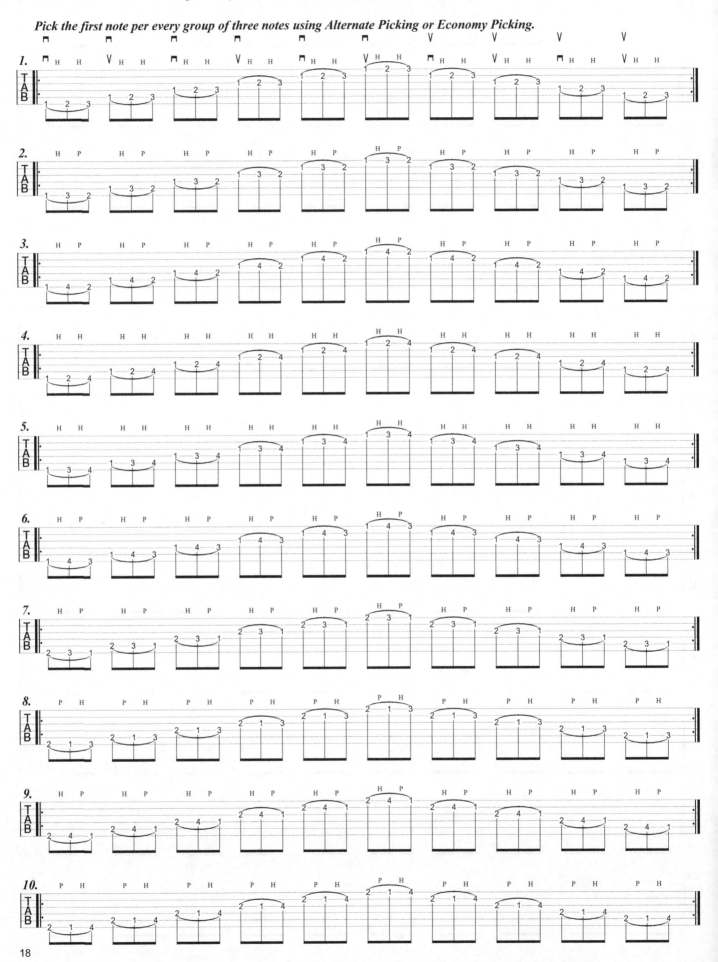

18

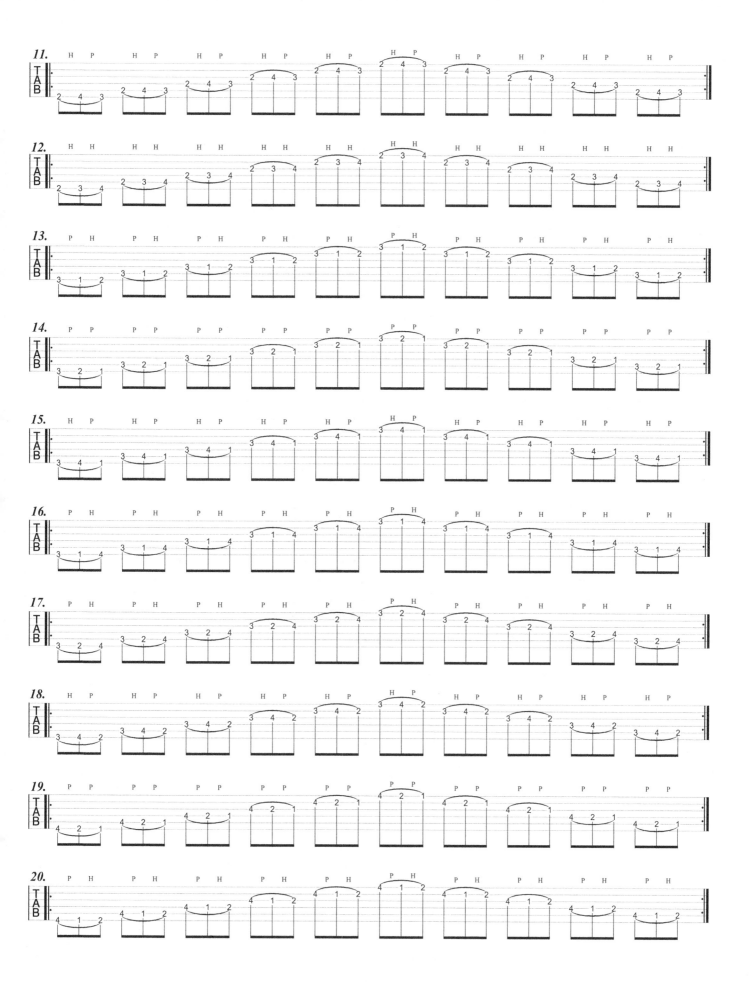

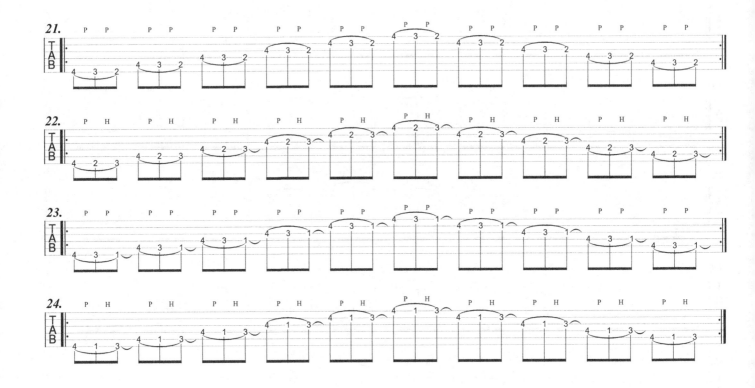

⇨ **Tip:** *Even though there are H's and P's above the frets to show hammer-ons or pull-offs, they are not necessary because the curved line shows hammer-ons or pull-offs. If the fret numbers are lower to higher, it's a hammer-on. If the numbers are higher to lower, it's a pull-off. Upcoming sections may only show the curved lines for hammer-ons or pull-offs.*

Three Fingers - Three Grouping

The hammer-on, pull-offs with alternate picking are especially challenging. Notice the picking pattern flips every measure in example #3.

21

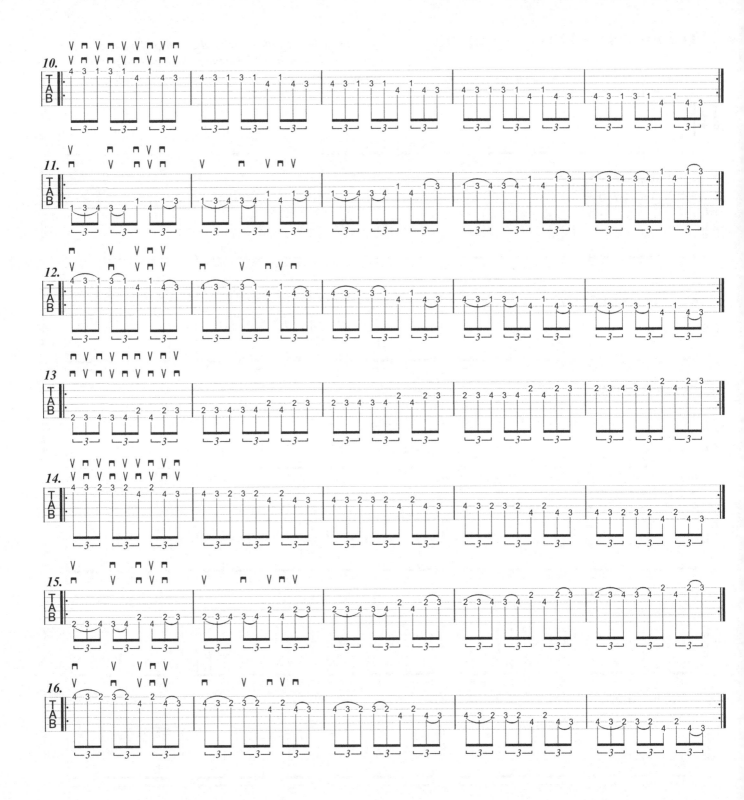

⇨ *Tip: One of the basic ideas of economy picking is to use as little motion as possible by never 'jumping' your pick over a string as in alternate picking. Another method for economy picking is to start with an up stroke when starting from the lowest string and a down stroke when starting from the first string. This keeps you on the 'inside' of the strings, and for some, it can add to your speed and accuracy. Try it out!*

Three Fingers - Four Grouping

Tip: Four grouping: up 4 notes from each note.

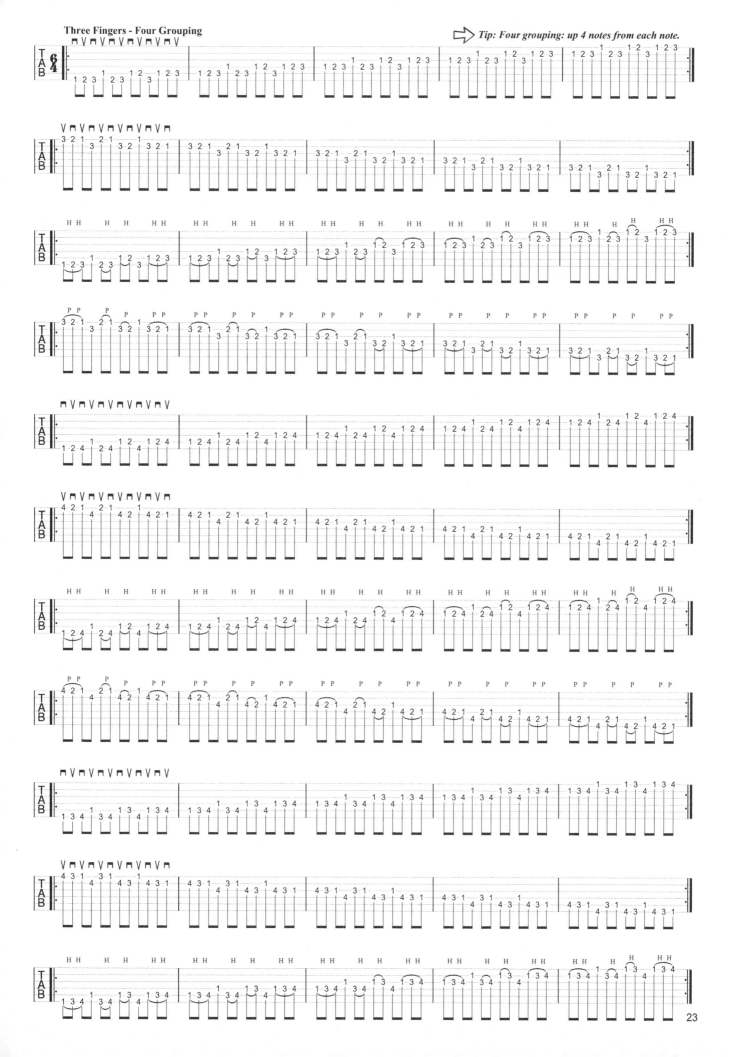

23

Economy picking when mixed with hammer-ons and pull-offs: A hammer-on or pull-off takes the place of a pick stroke. This means that if you pick down and then hammer on, your next pick could be up or down. When in doubt, alternate!

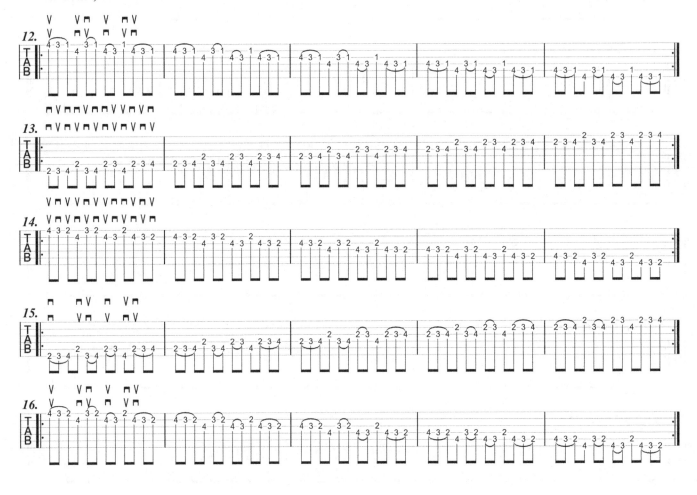

Four Fingers

These are arguably some of the most important exercises for the guitar because all four fingers are used with every combination.

Use moderate pressure when pressing the strings down with your fretting hand. When playing these exercises and other exercises in this book, you should try playing with your fretting fingers as close to the strings as possible, only pressing with enough pressure to produce a clear sound.

When picking, it is also best to use moderate pressure. But picking should also be practiced lightly, almost brushing the top of each string and then try bearing down or picking a little harder for variation and feel.

These types of exercises also help with randomizing notes within chromatic lines when soloing or playing riffs.

⇨ *Tip: It is difficult to get the pinky to stay close to the strings. This is because the tendons for the ring finger and pinky join together, making it difficult for these fingers to act independently. You will notice that, with many guitarists, their pinky finger sticks up higher off the strings than their other fingers. This happens because the pinky is 'helping' the ring finger lift.*
Here is a great exercise to help gain independence, strengthen the ring finger, and get the pinky down:
To begin, place all four fingers on a single string at the 5th fret, each finger on its own fret. Next, lift and press only your ring finger while keeping the other fingers lightly pressed. Repeat 10 times. Do this on other frets and strings all over the neck.

Alternate pick and remember to play from different frets.

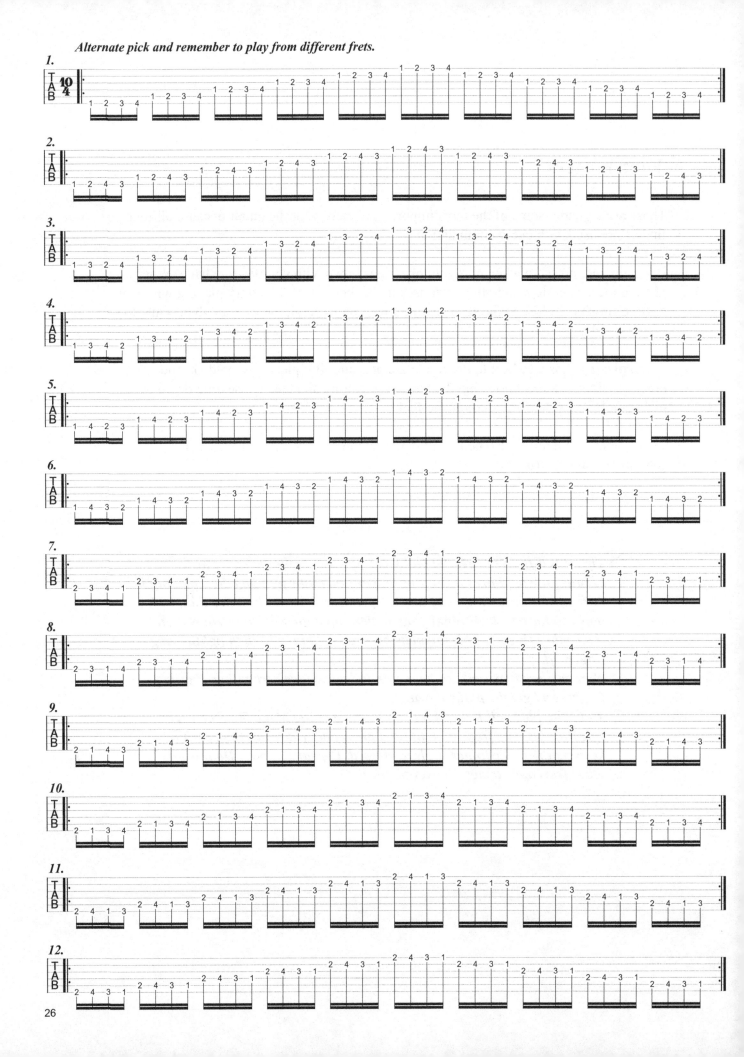

26

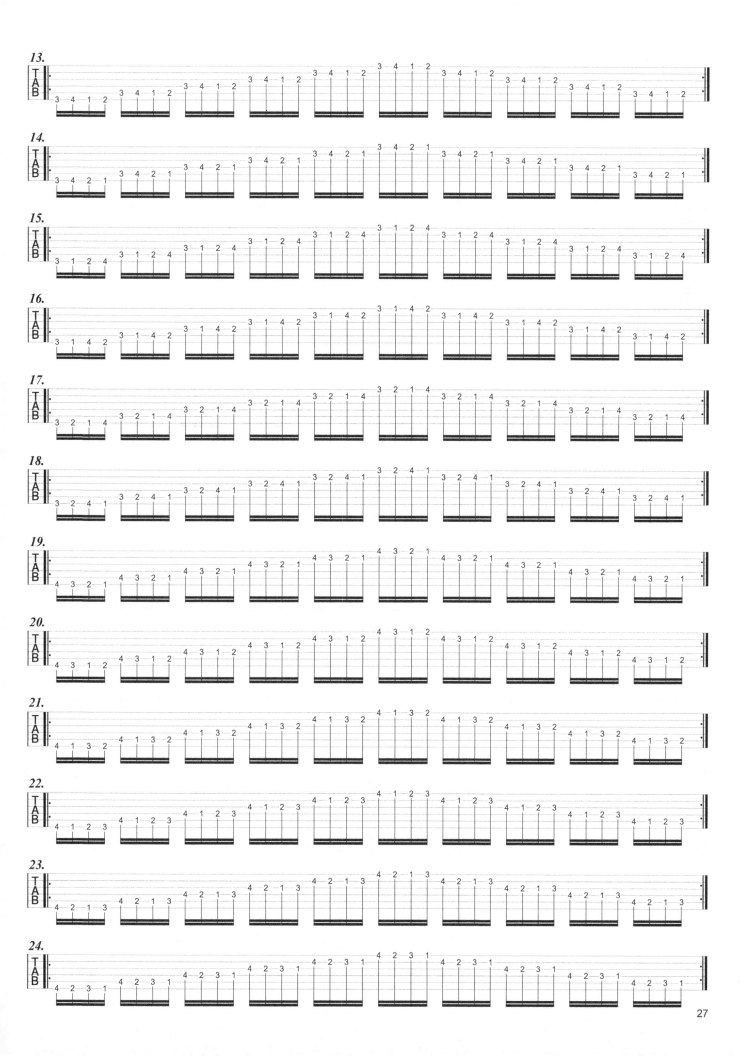

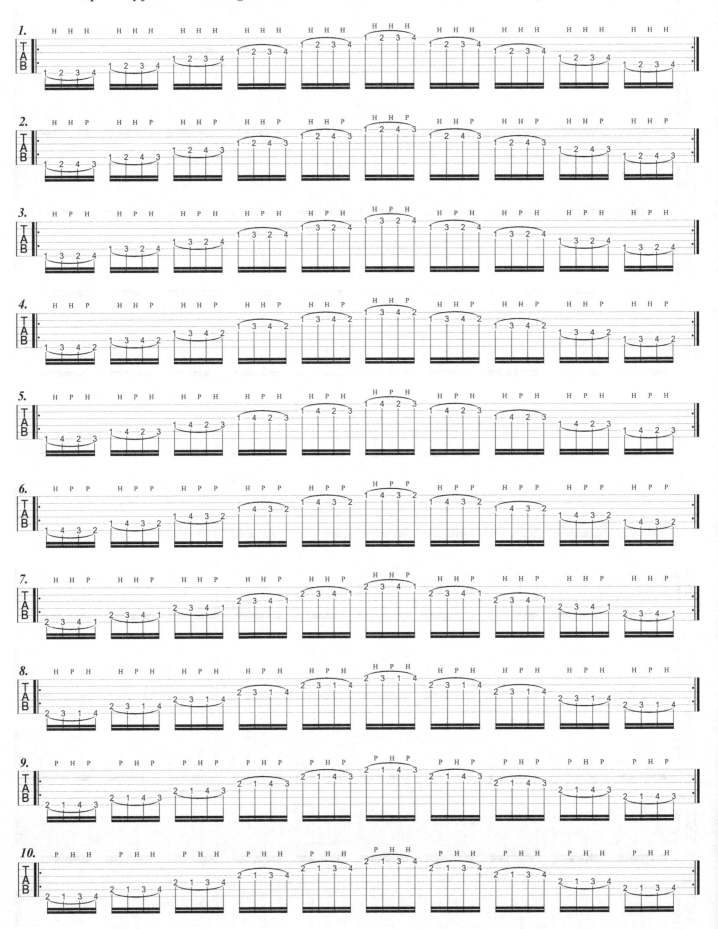

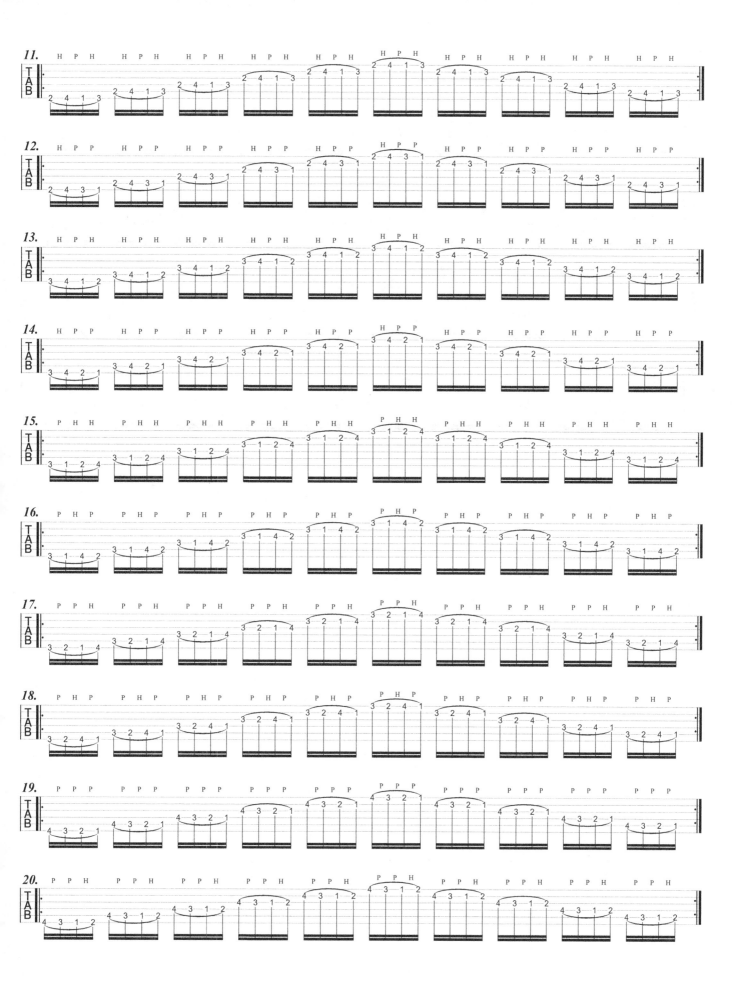

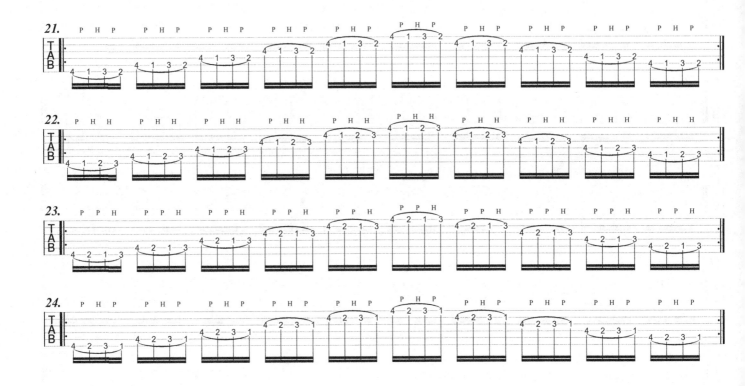

Alternate Picking

In this first example, alternate picking is shown as strict down-up. The second line shows alternate picking as up-down, reversing the pattern. Exercises should be done both ways for best results.

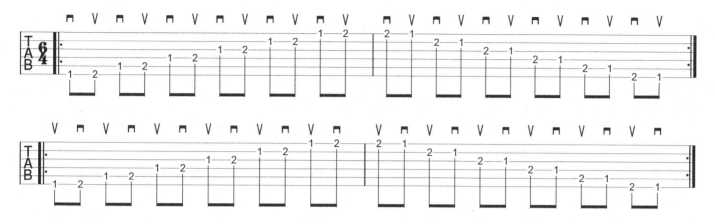

Alternate picking with hammer-ons and pull-offs. You may alternate your pick even though there is a hammer-on or pull-off between them.

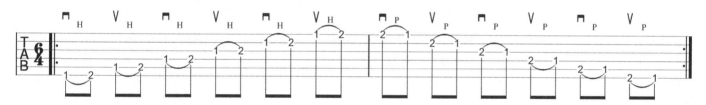

With three notes per string, alternate picking will switch between **outside picking** and **inside picking**. Outside picking: When switching strings, picking occurs on the outside of the strings. When switching strings, picking occurs on the inside of the strings.

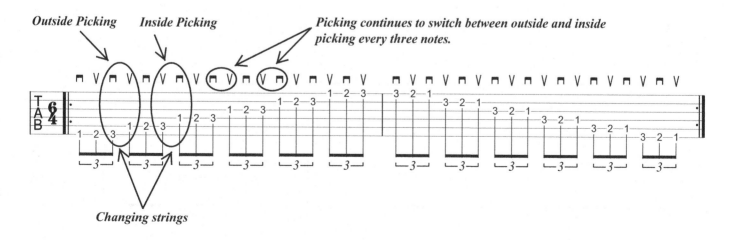

Outside Picking   *Inside Picking*   *Picking continues to switch between outside and inside picking every three notes.*

Changing strings

Economy Picking

The idea is to use as little movement as possible in the picking hand by avoiding jumping over a string before picking it. In alternate picking, after picking D U D, you would *hop* over the next string and pick U D U. With economy picking, the pick stroke continues to the next string in the same direction you are heading; *inside picking* is used if starting with an up pick.

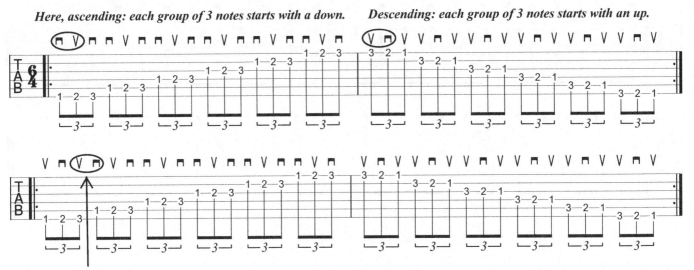

Because this example starts with an up pick, the sequence is reversed only for the first three notes, creating a moment of inside picking, and then continues the picking sequence as in the first example.

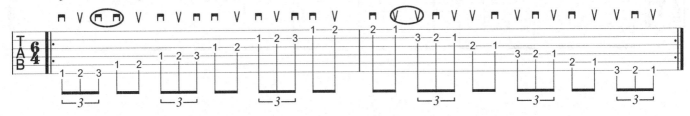

Sometimes the picking sequence can be interrupted with a hammer-on or pull-off. It doesn't matter; continue picking in the same direction that you are heading across the strings.

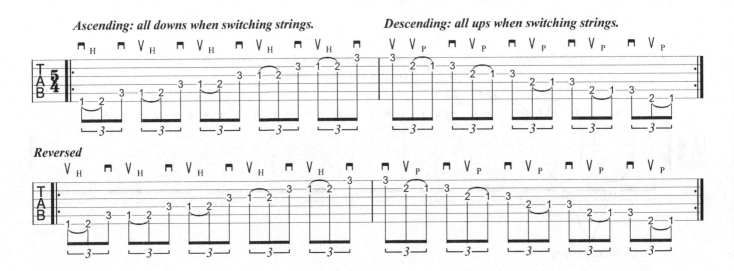

Four Fingers - Three Grouping

This exercise is quite challenging. It takes a lot of finger control, but if you have been doing the earlier four finger exercises, you'll find this one is a lot of fun once you get used to the pattern. When ascending, three grouping is up three notes from each note. Descending is three notes down from each note. Take it slow, try a metronome, and play the exercise from many different frets.

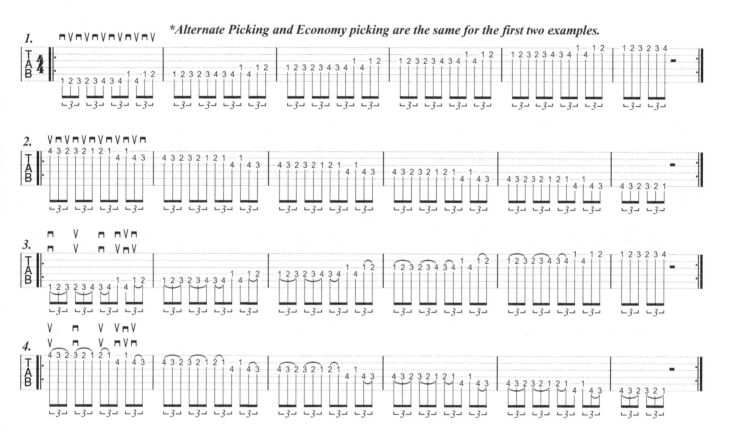

Four Fingers - Four Grouping

These exercises are similar to the three grouping exercises, but more challenging. When ascending, the four grouping is up four notes from each note. Descending is four notes down from each note. Take it slow, try a metronome, and move the exercises to different frets.

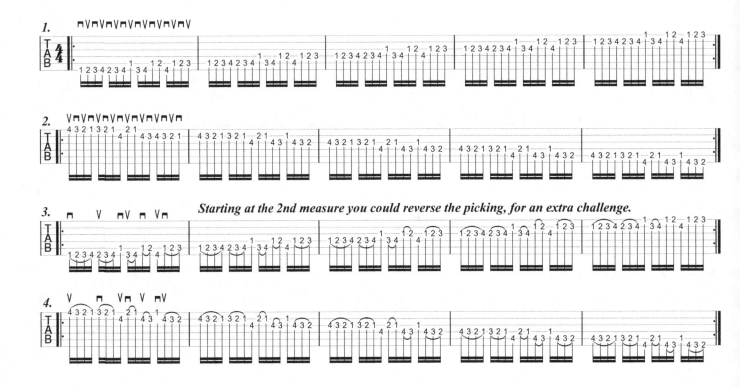

Two and Three Fingers

This section combines the two-finger patterns with the three-finger patterns. Most combinations are included! Often times, in guitar playing, you will have to traverse the strings with two to three notes, two to four notes, or even three to four notes. Think blues scales, chromatic passages mixed within scales, or just thousands and thousands of riffs. These combination exercises will make you very versatile and greatly increase accuracy and control for both hands. Exercises may be flipped by starting from the first string and descending to the sixth string.

Take your time by picking one exercise per practice session or running through a whole page. Sections are organized and numbered to help you keep track of which exercises you are working on. The exercises are not necessarily organized from easiest to most difficult.

Read below before continuing:

The upcoming sections are very large, with the exercises showing fingering without hammer-ons and pull-offs. If these examples were added to this book, this book would be enormous! At some point, redo the exercises, adding hammer-ons, pull-offs, alternate picking, or economy picking.

Tip: Another idea would be to apply 3 grouping or 4 grouping to the upcoming two and three finger patterns!

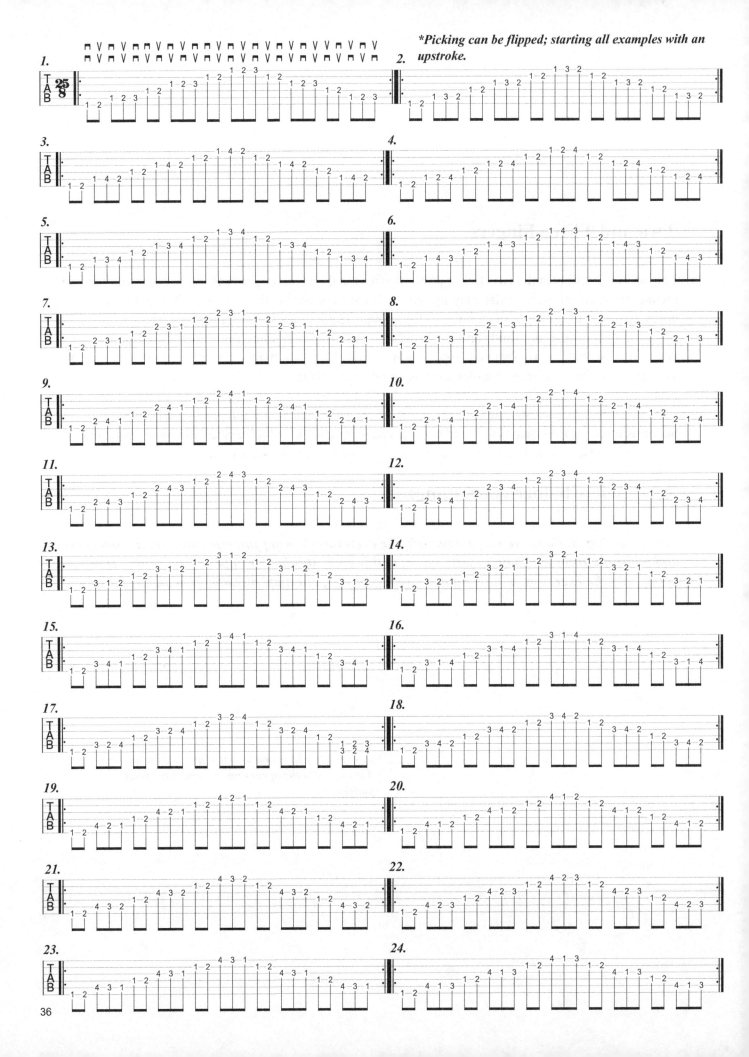

Picking can be flipped; starting all examples with an upstroke.

Remember examples can be replayed with hammer-ons and pull-offs.

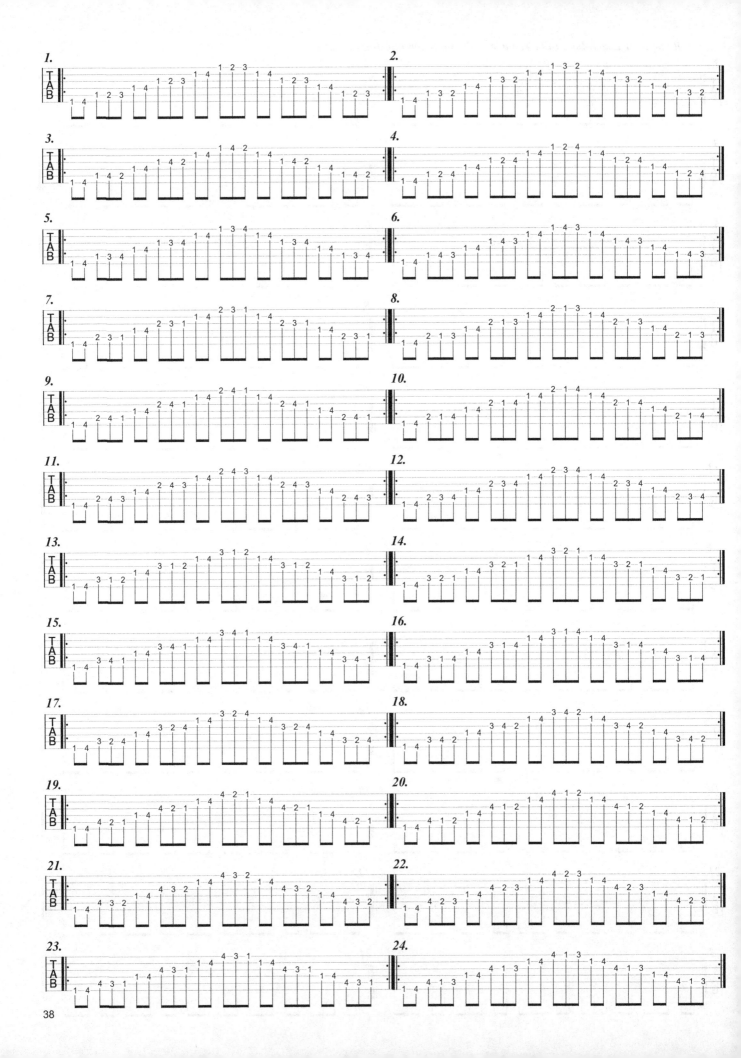

38

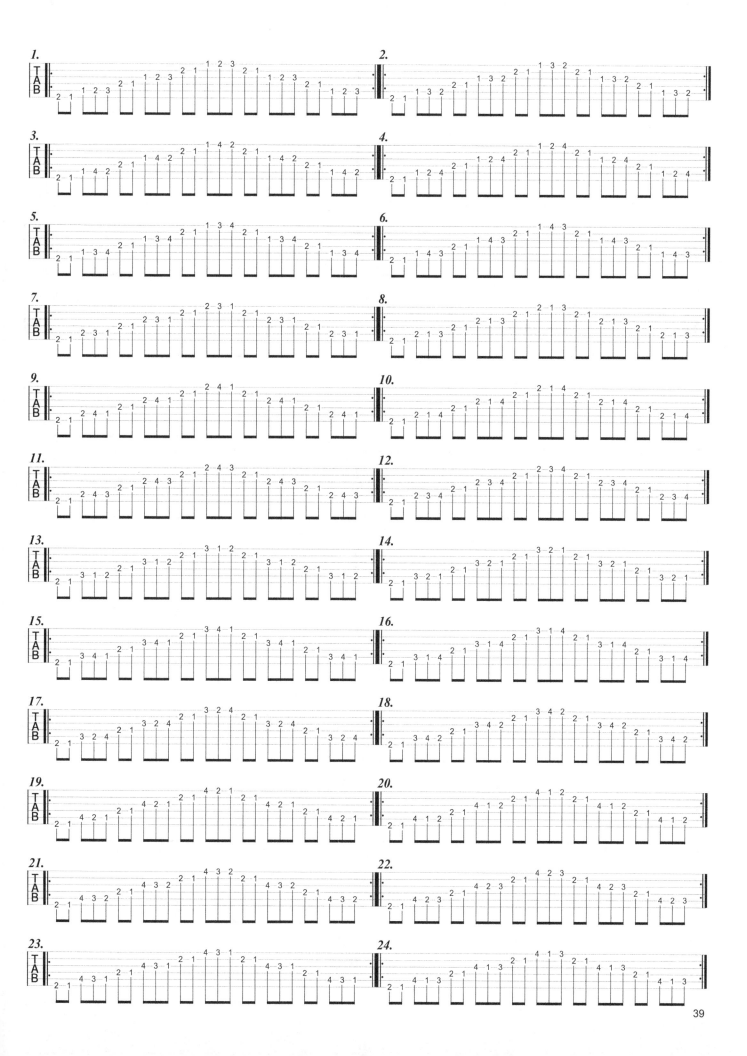

39

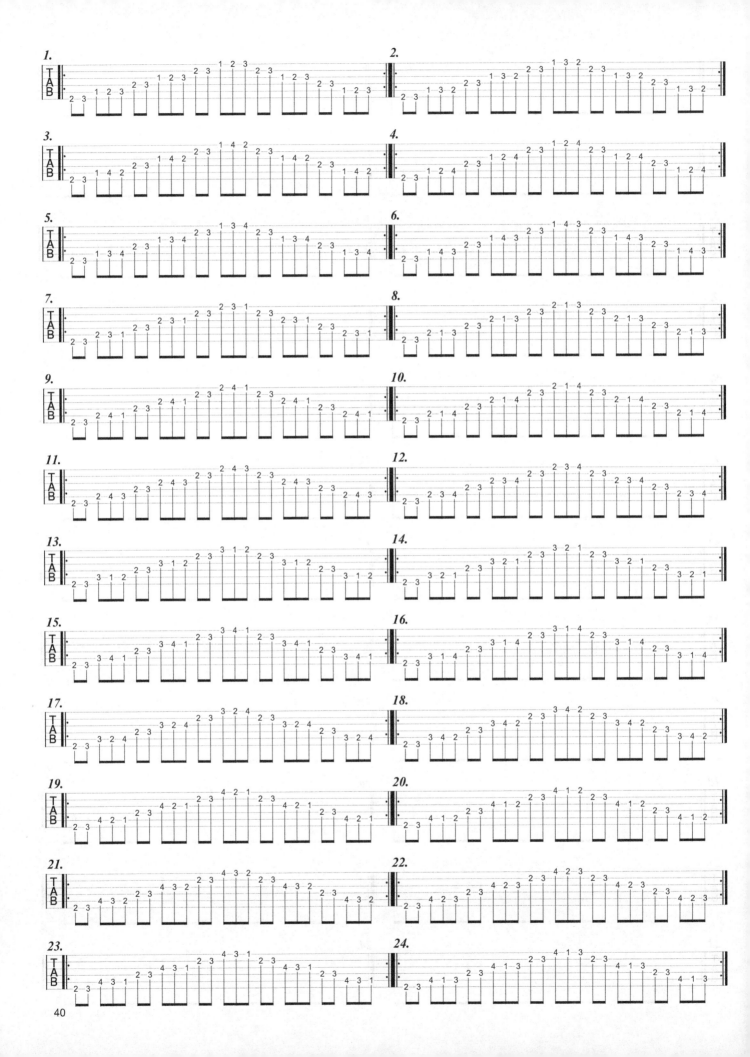

40

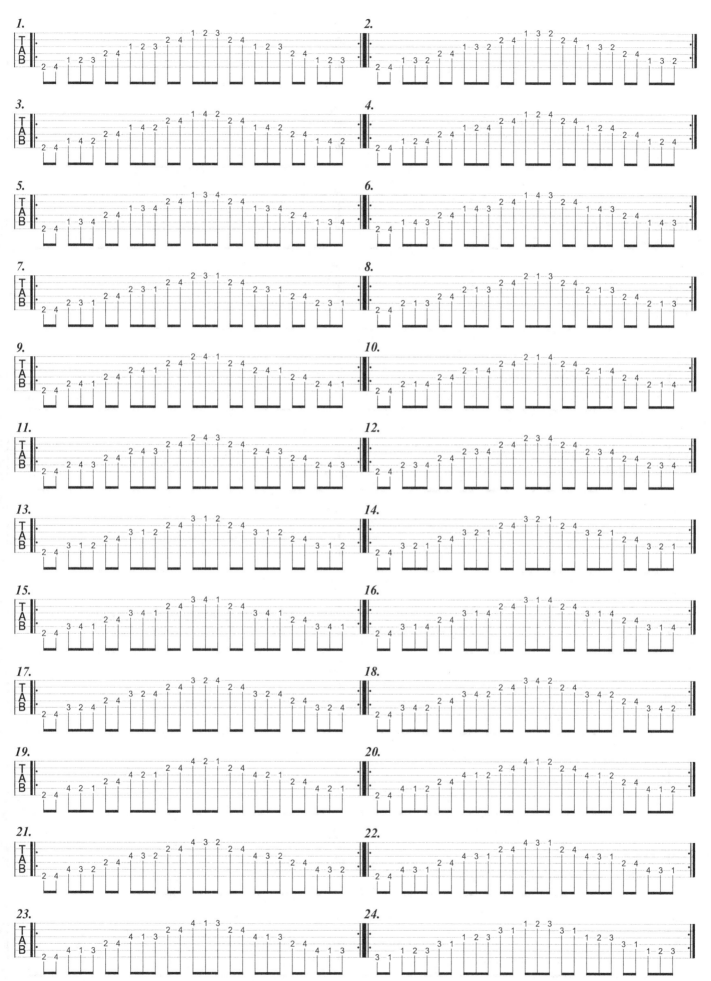

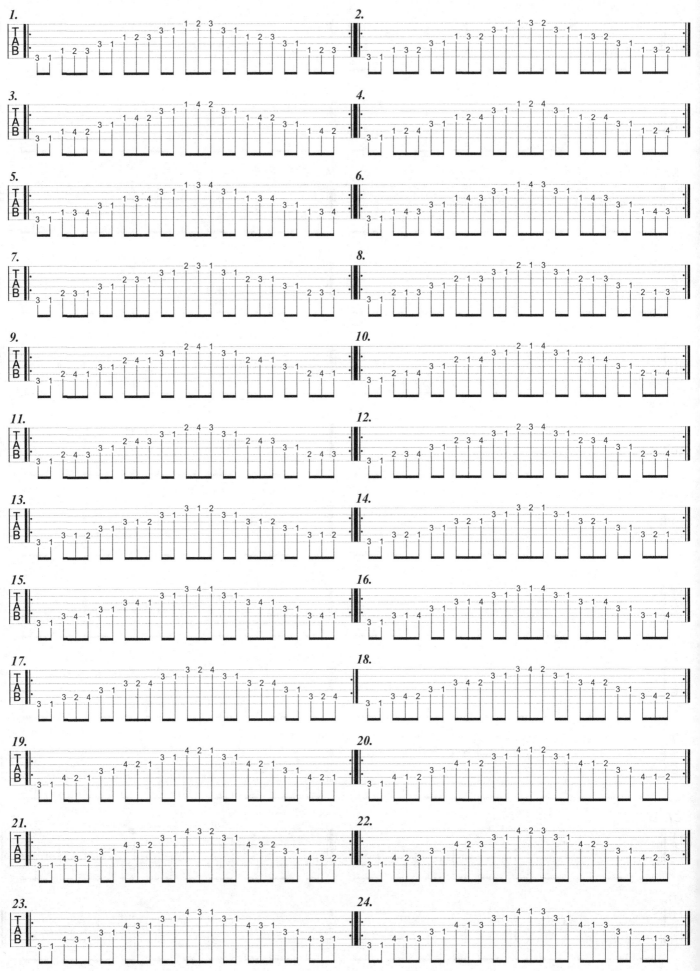

42

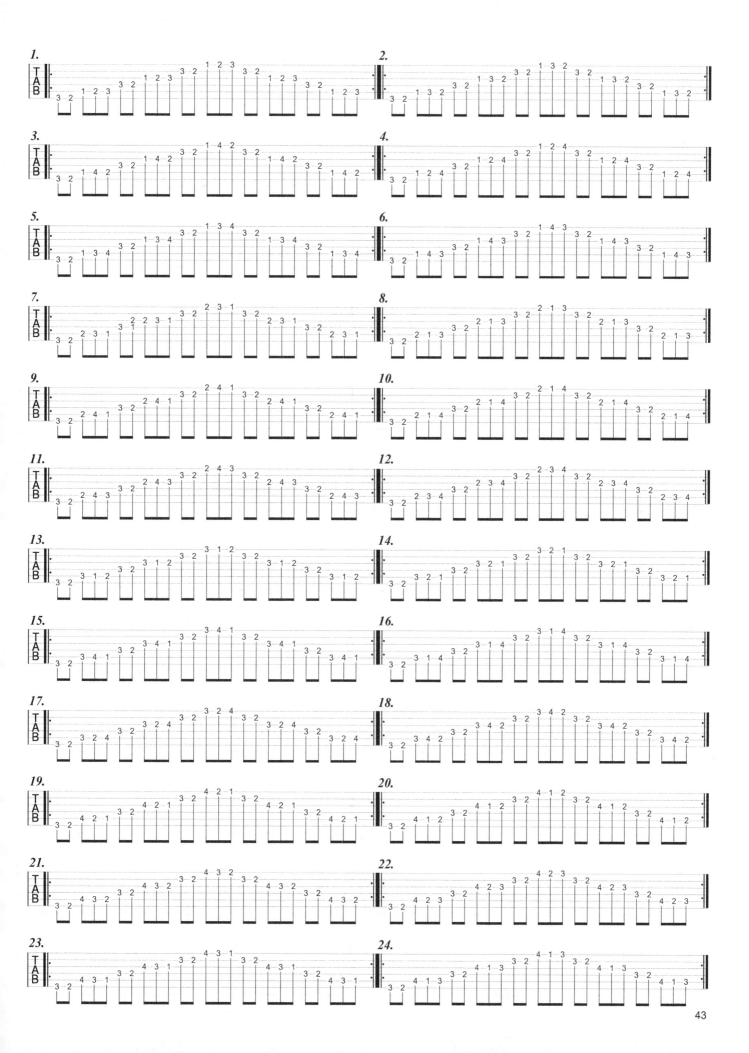

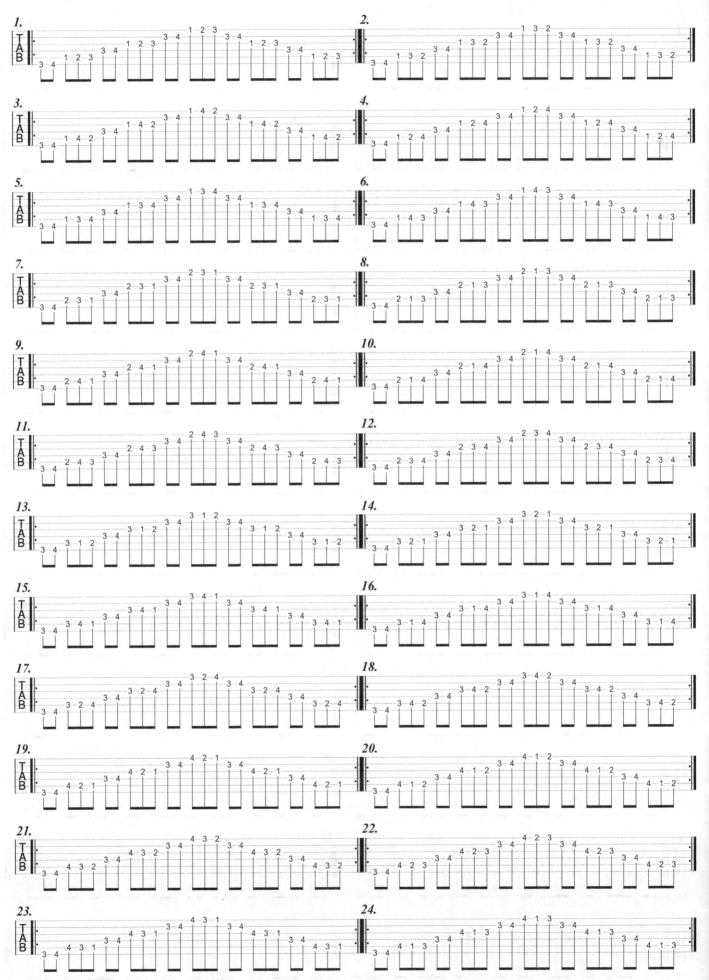

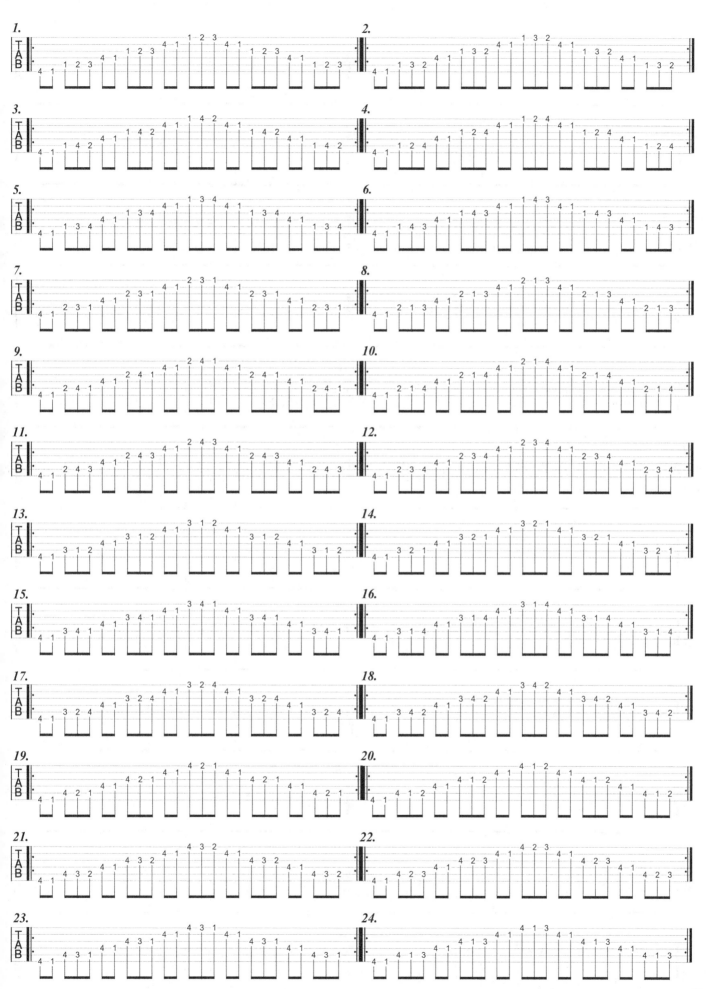

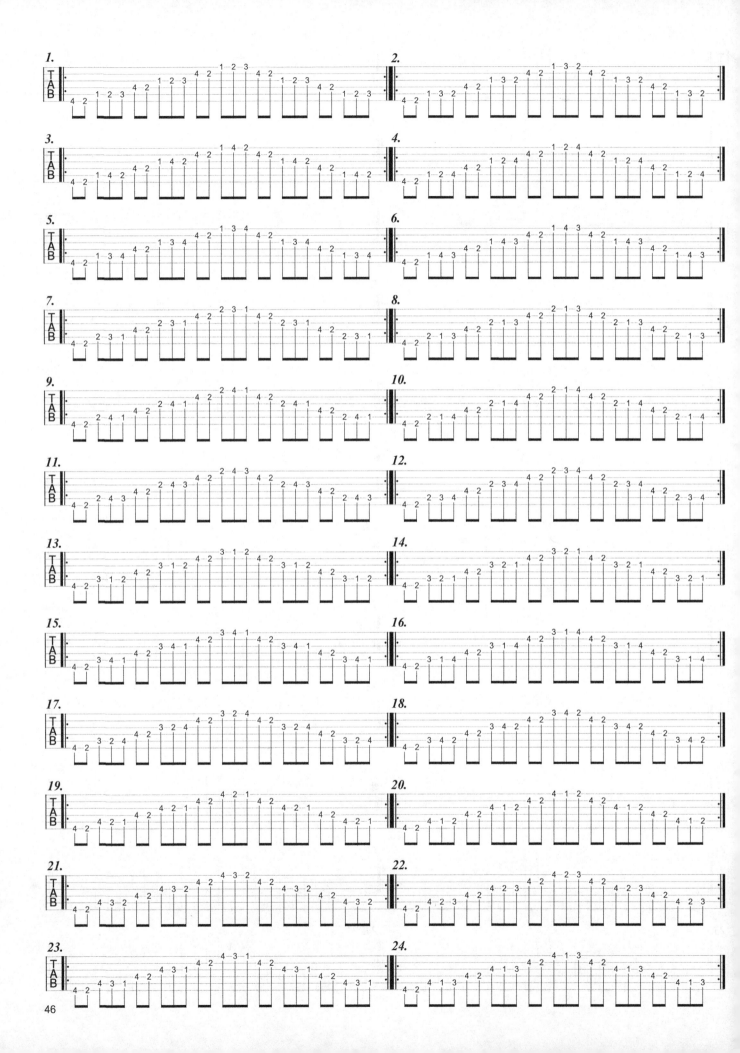

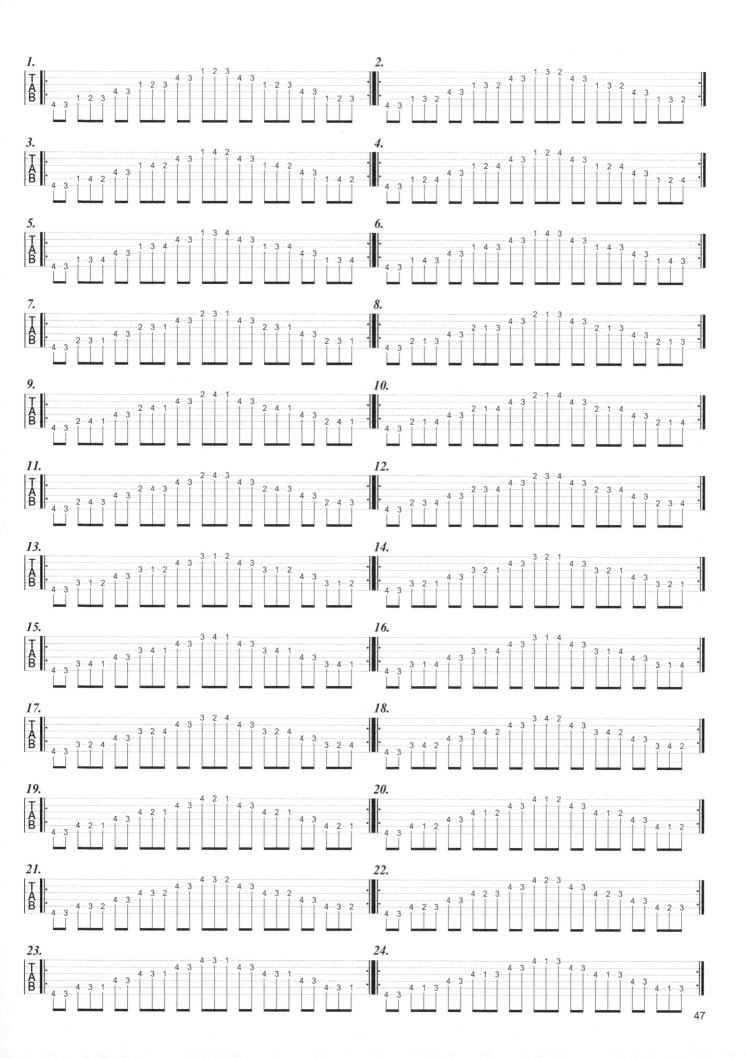

Two and Four Fingers

Alternate pick throughout. Redo all of the exercises with hammer-ons and pull-offs.

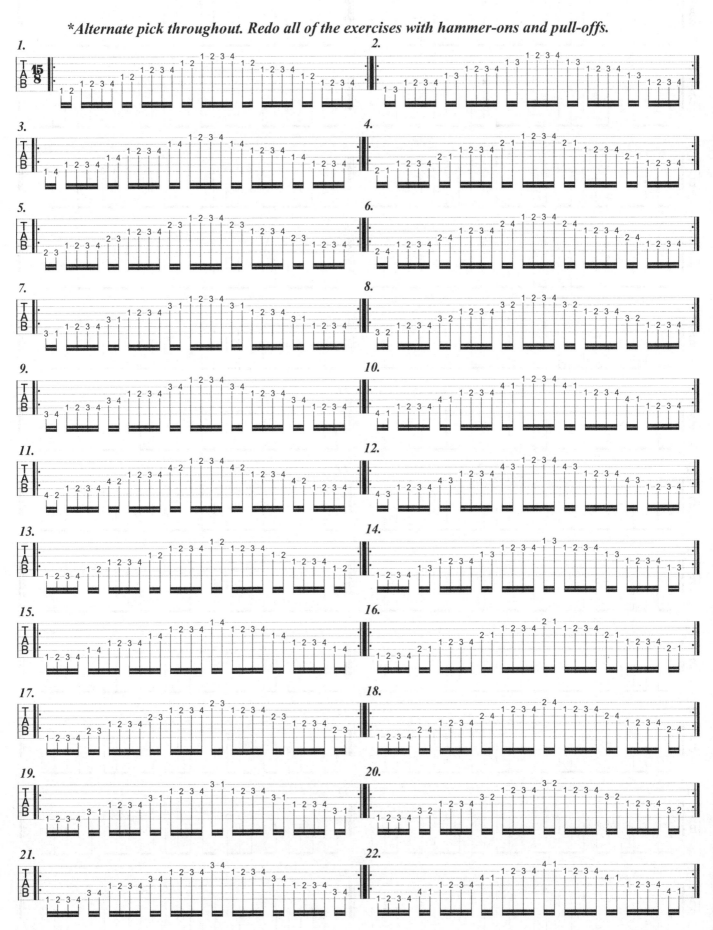

48

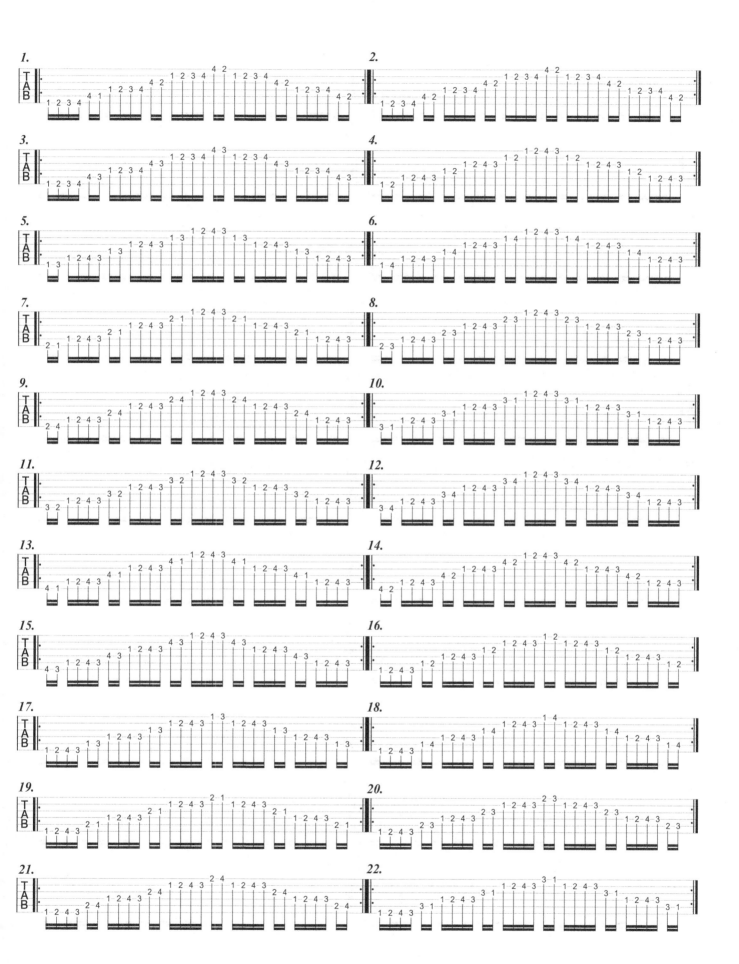

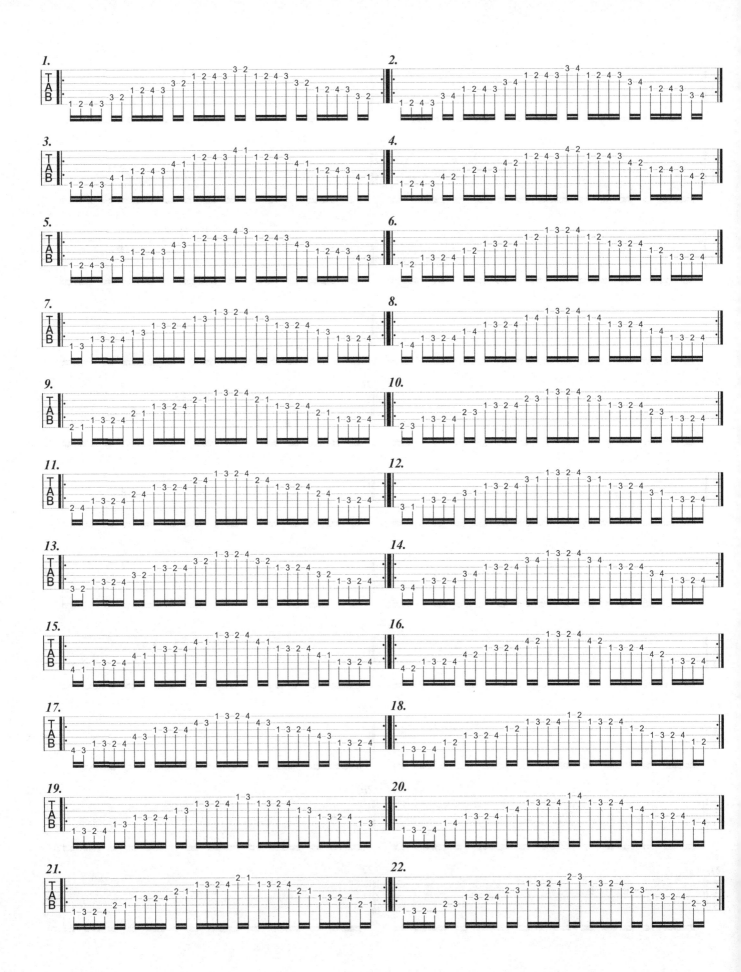

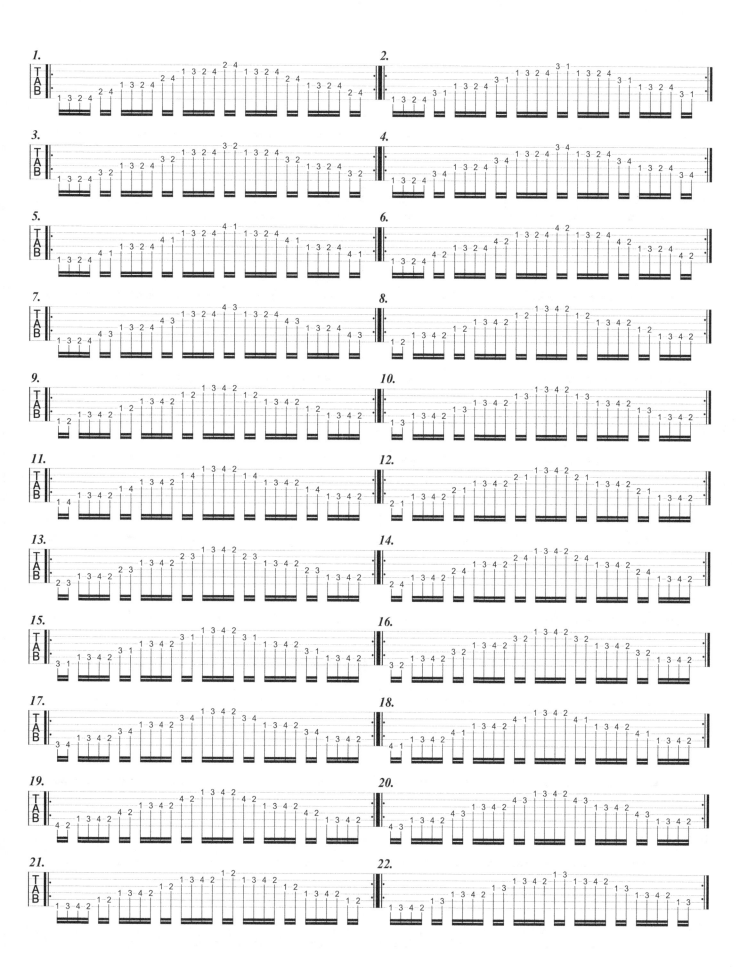

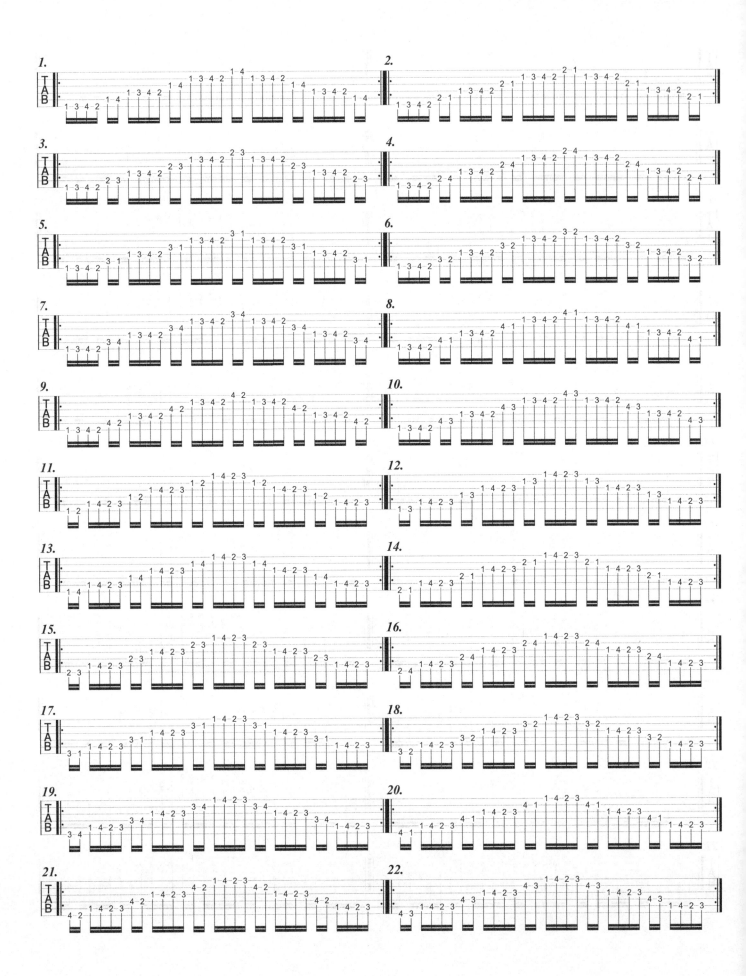

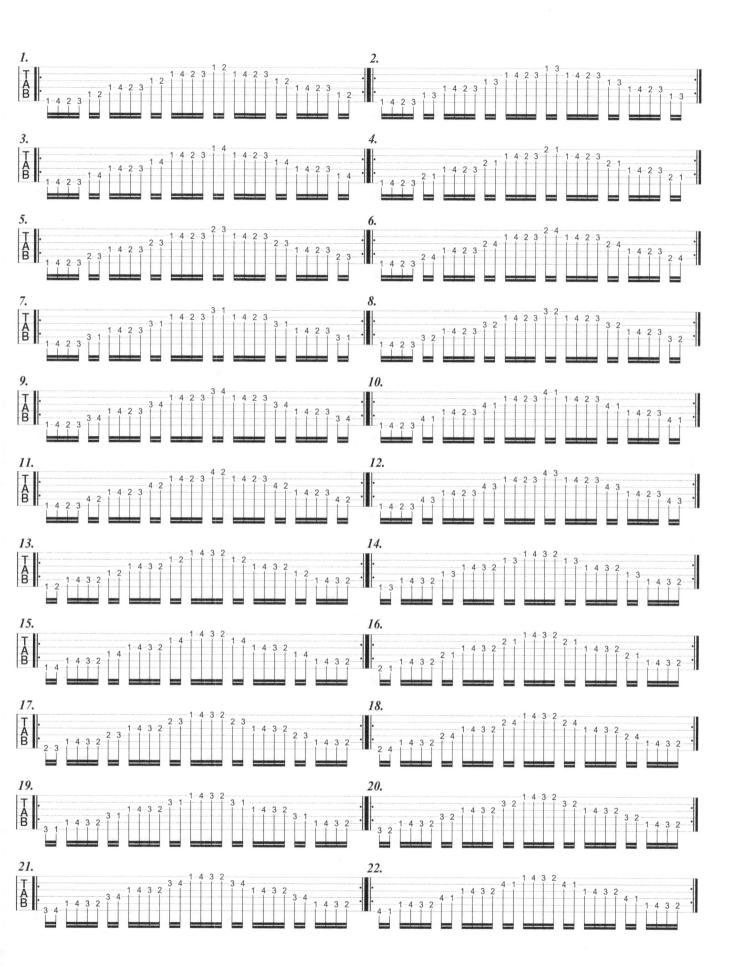

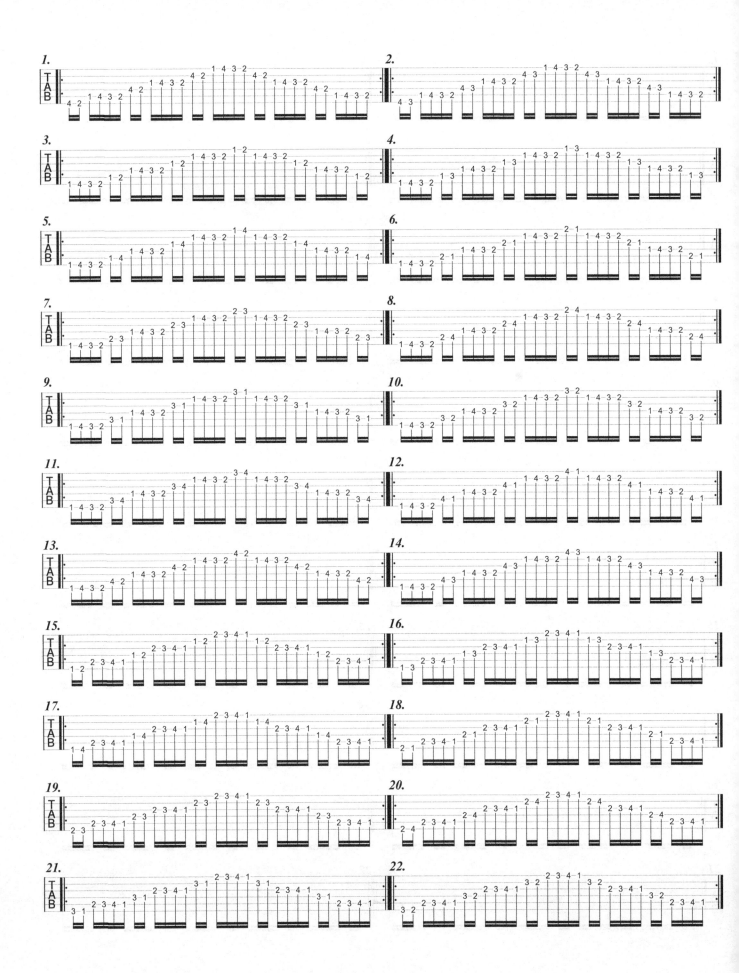

54

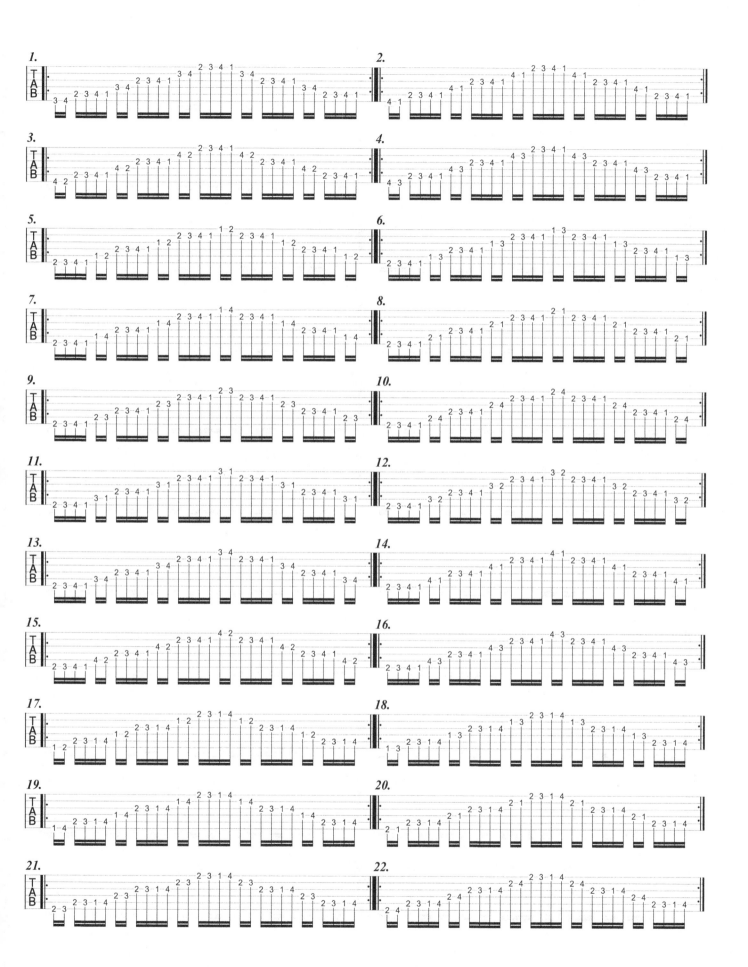

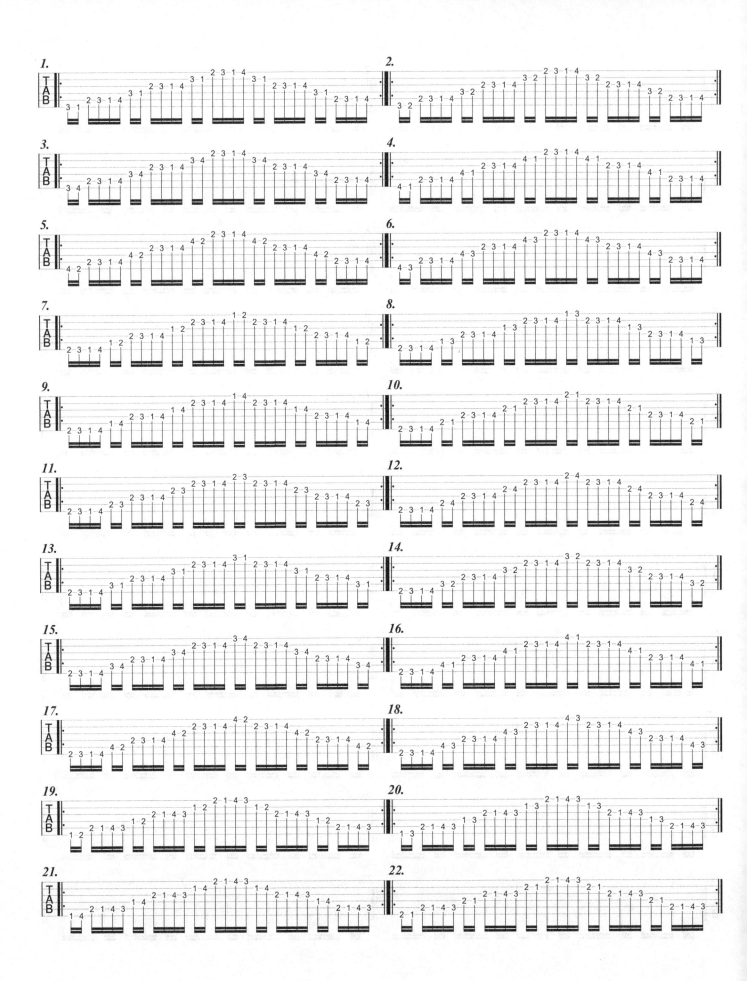

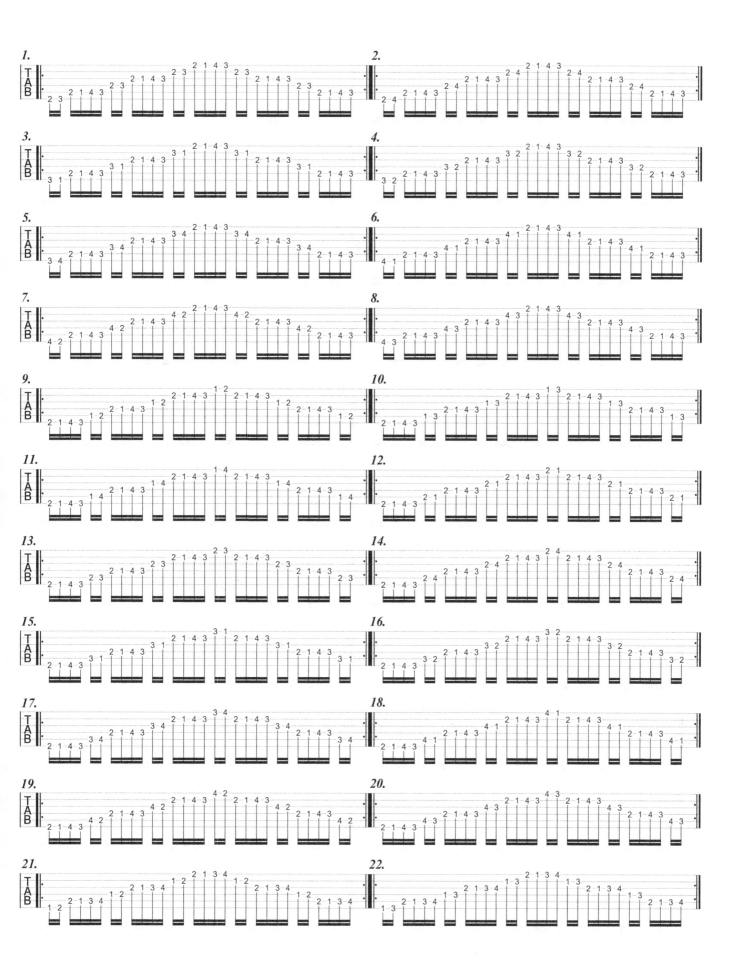

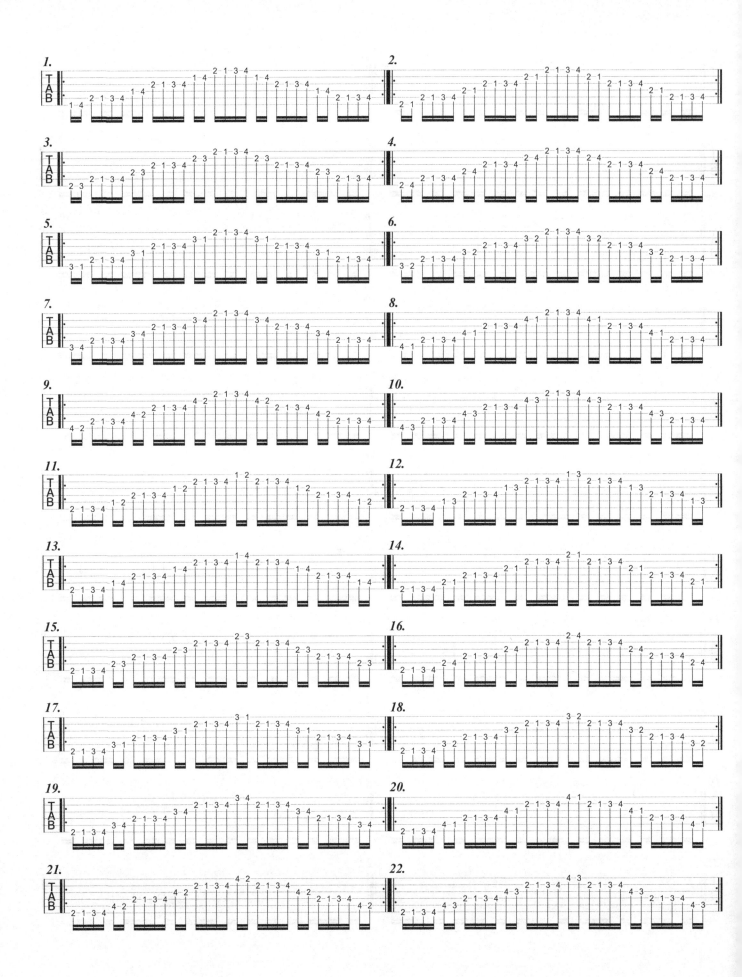

58

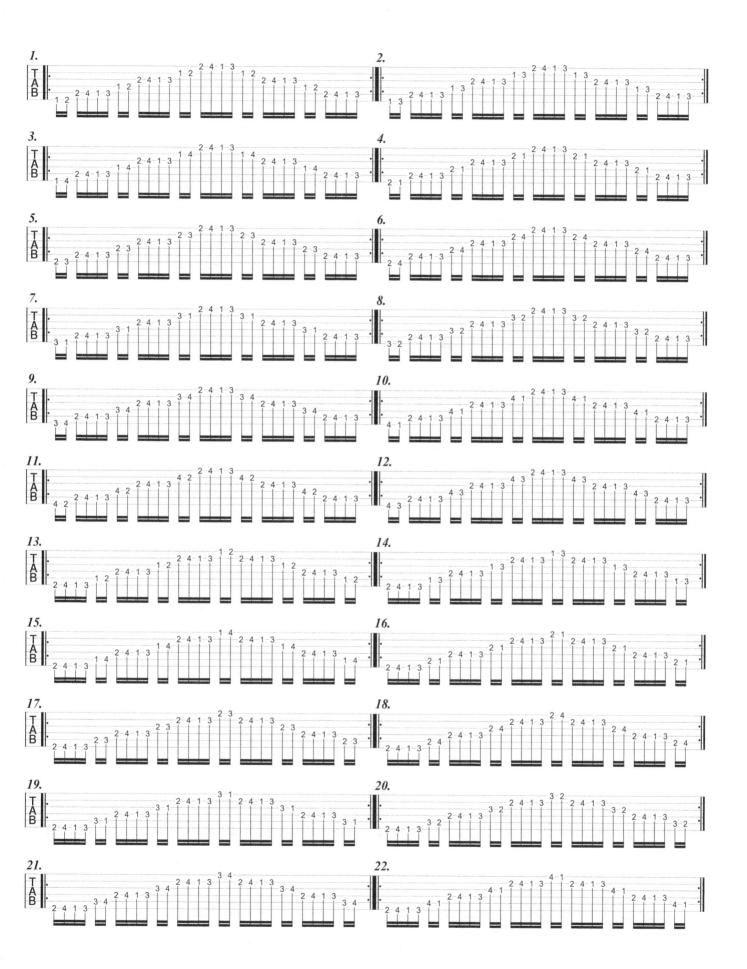

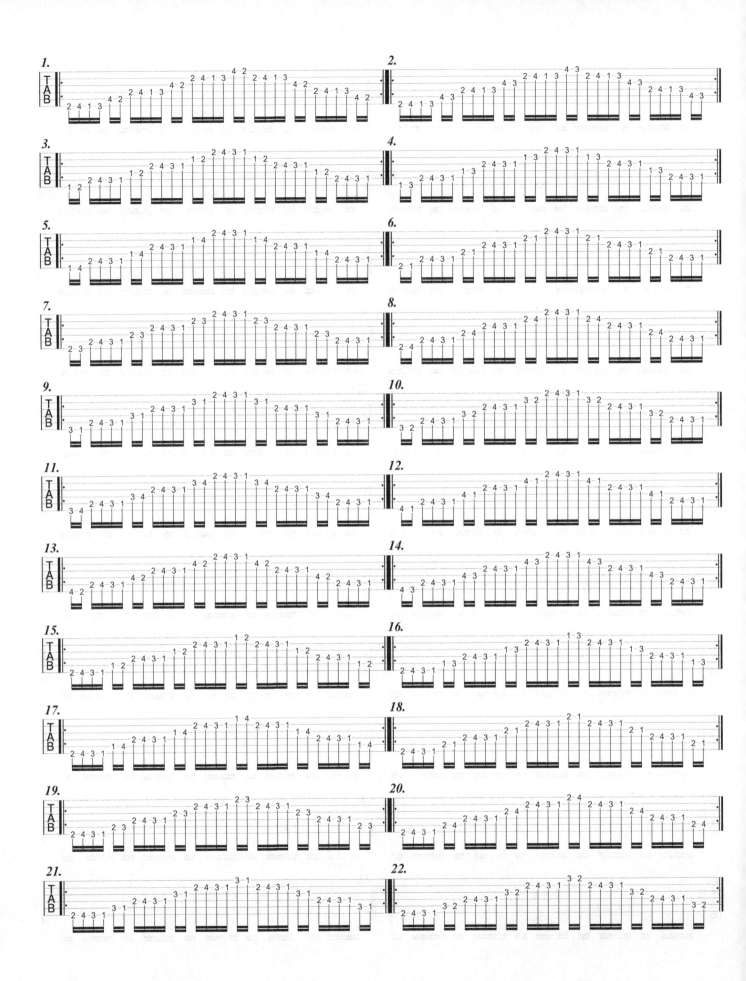

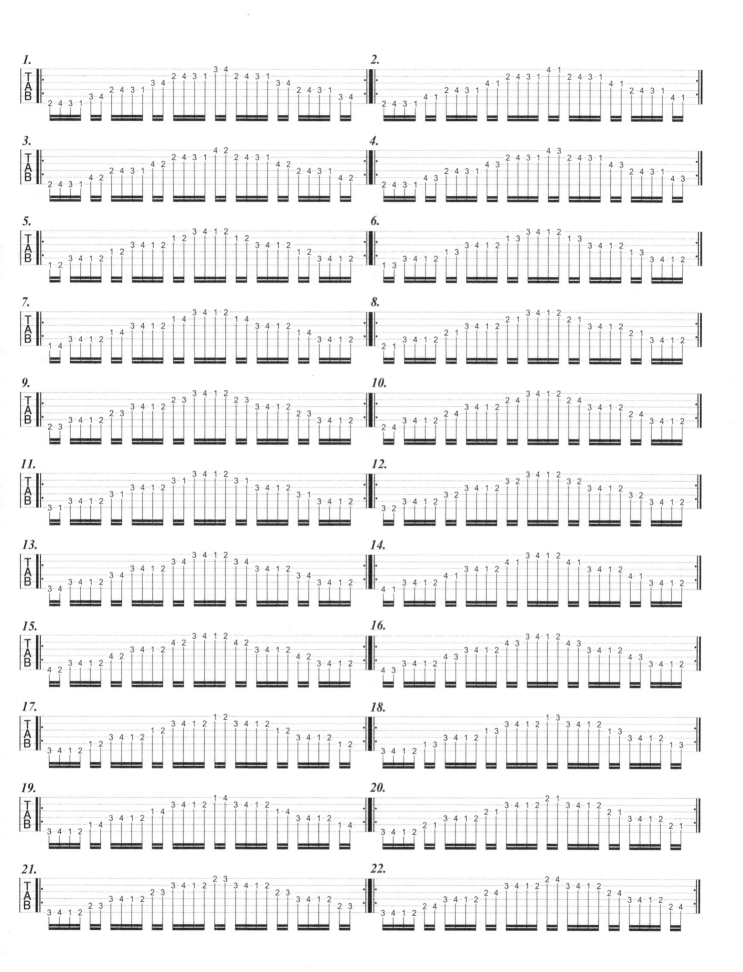

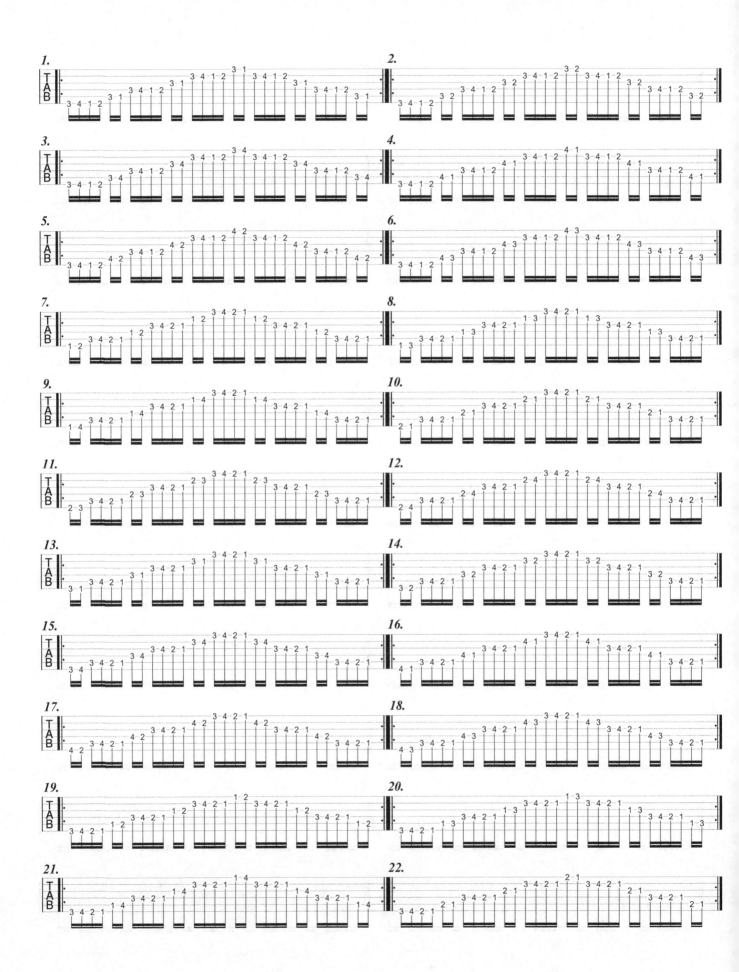

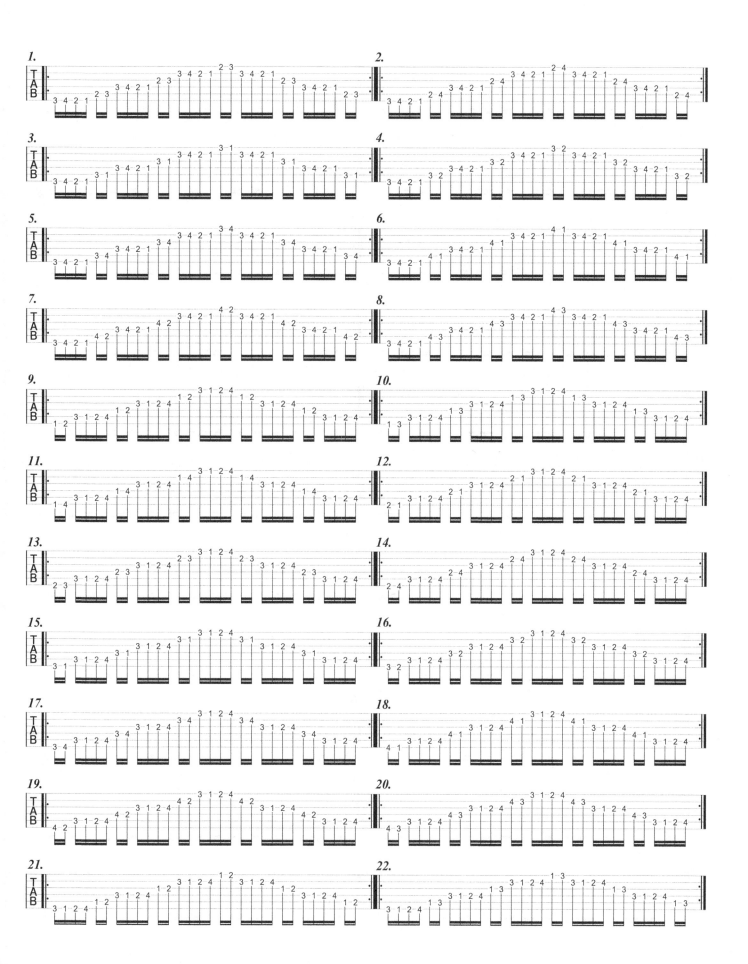

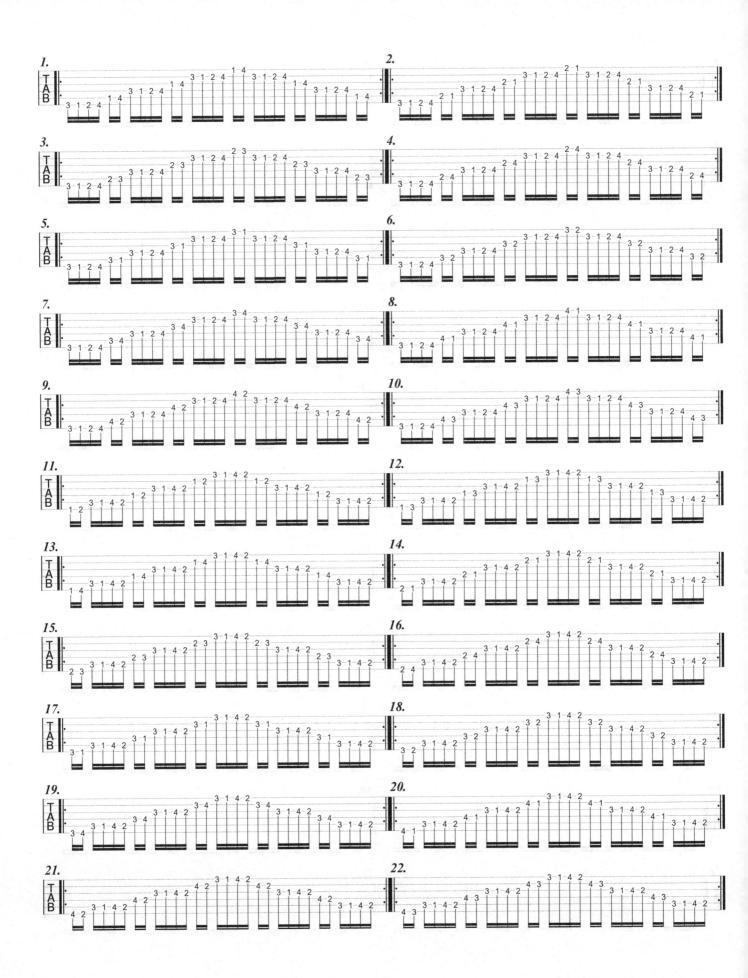

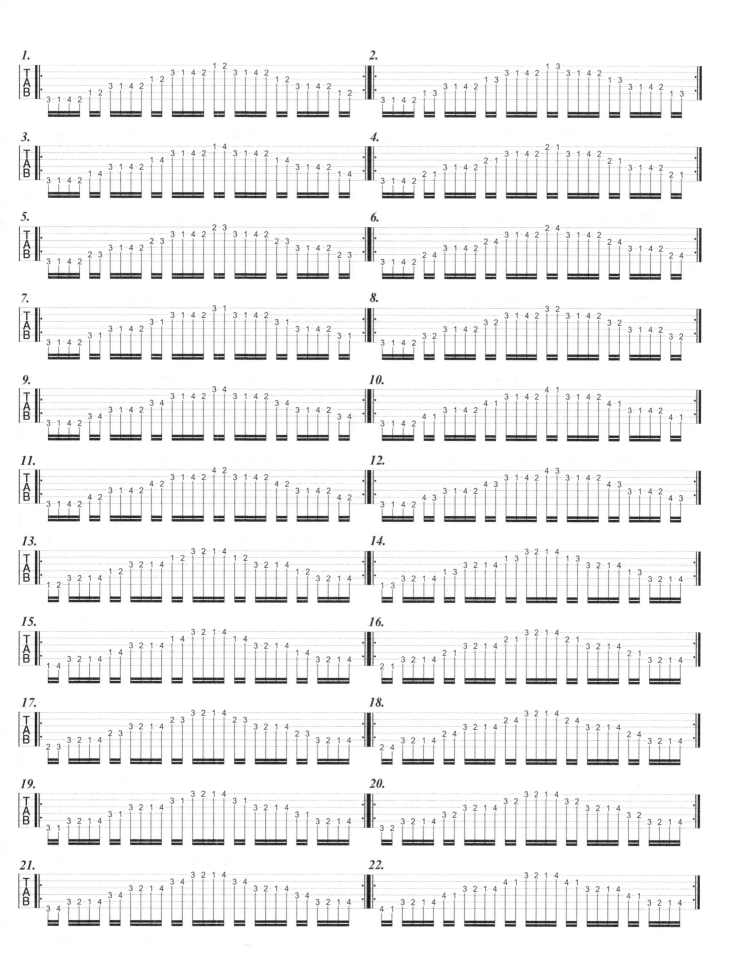

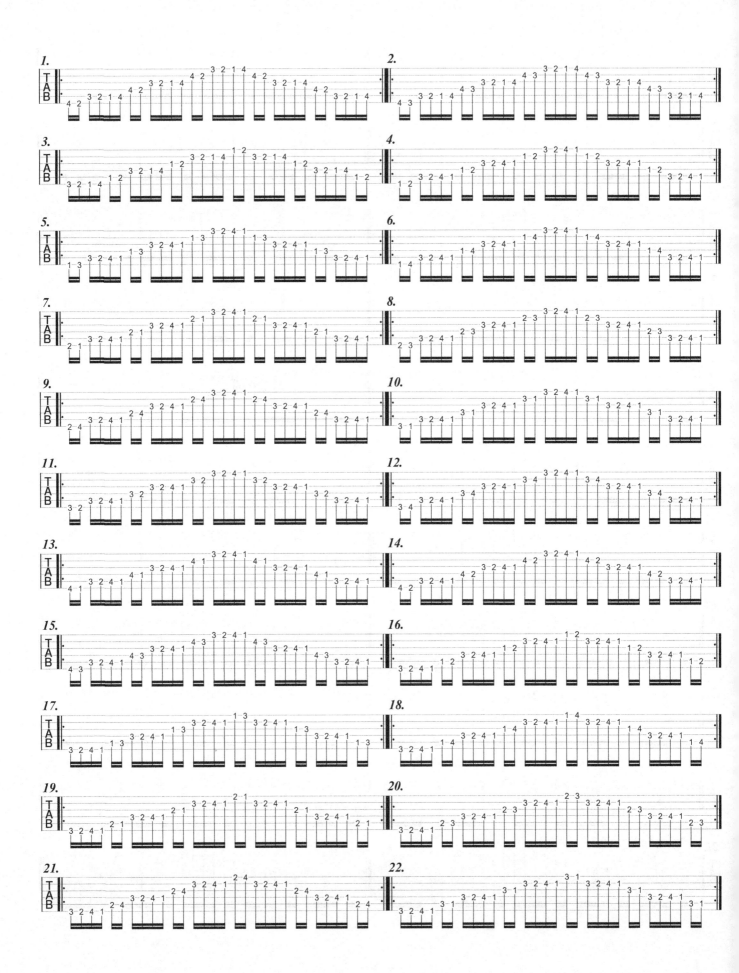

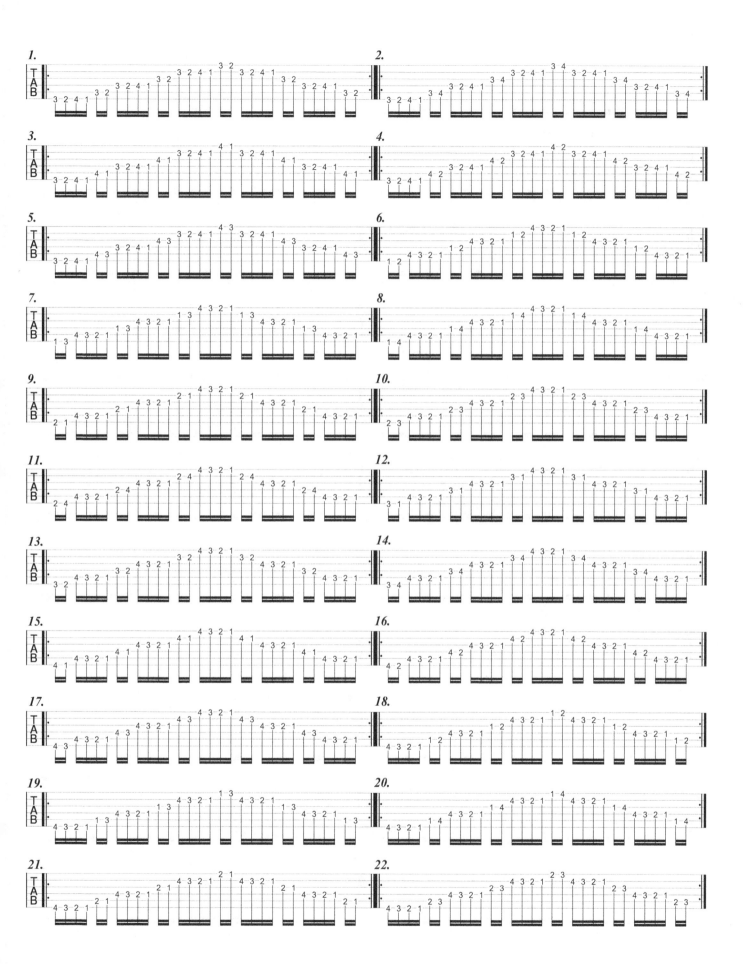

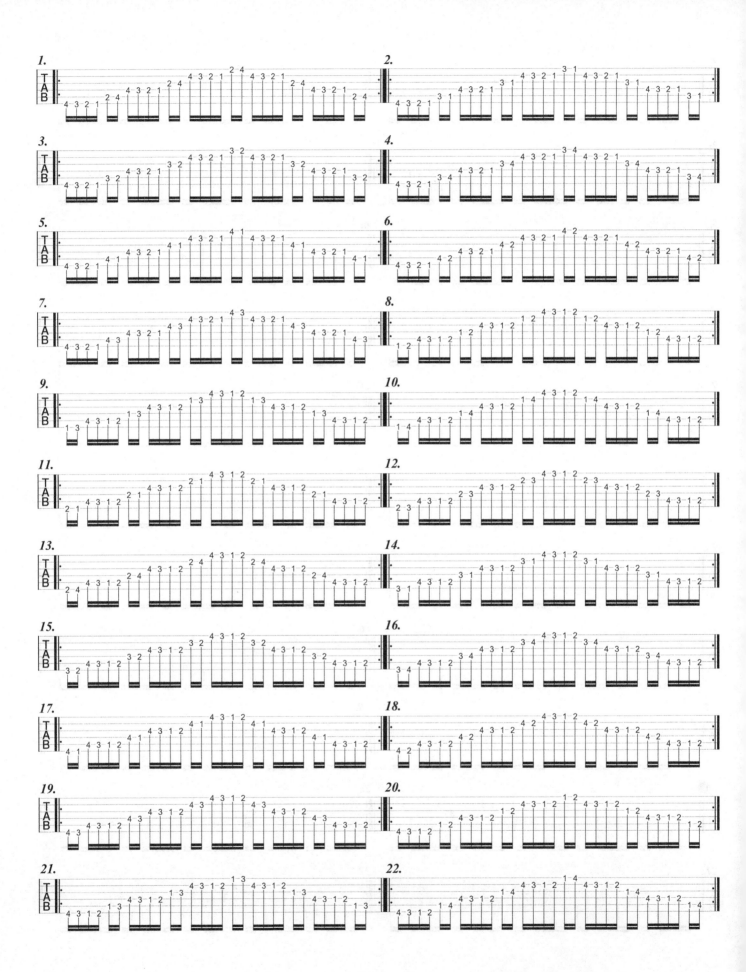

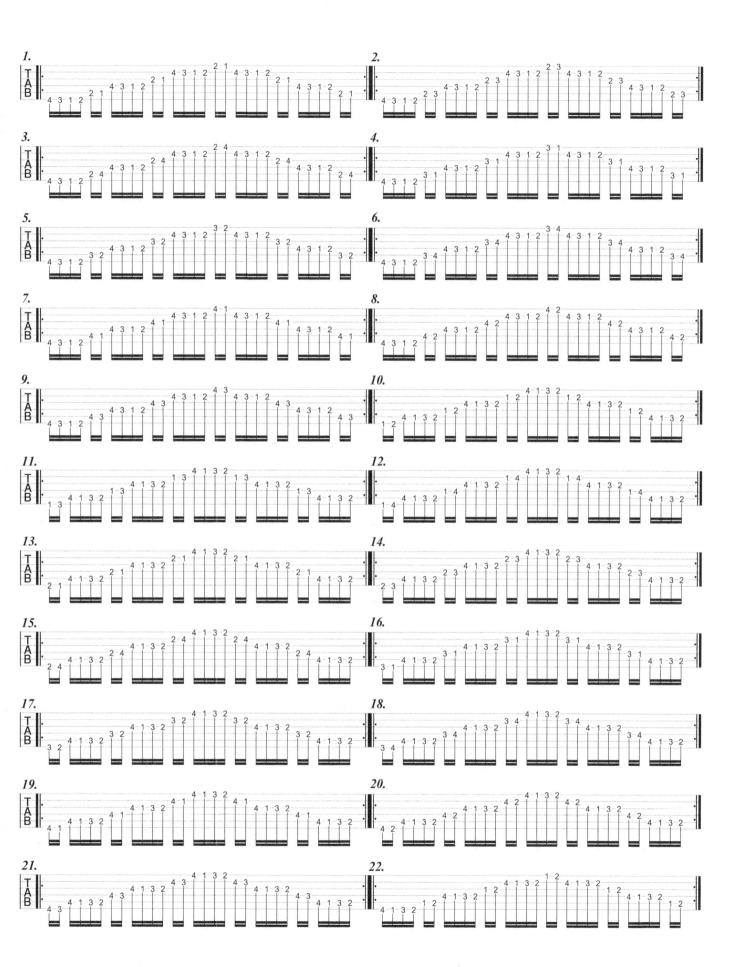

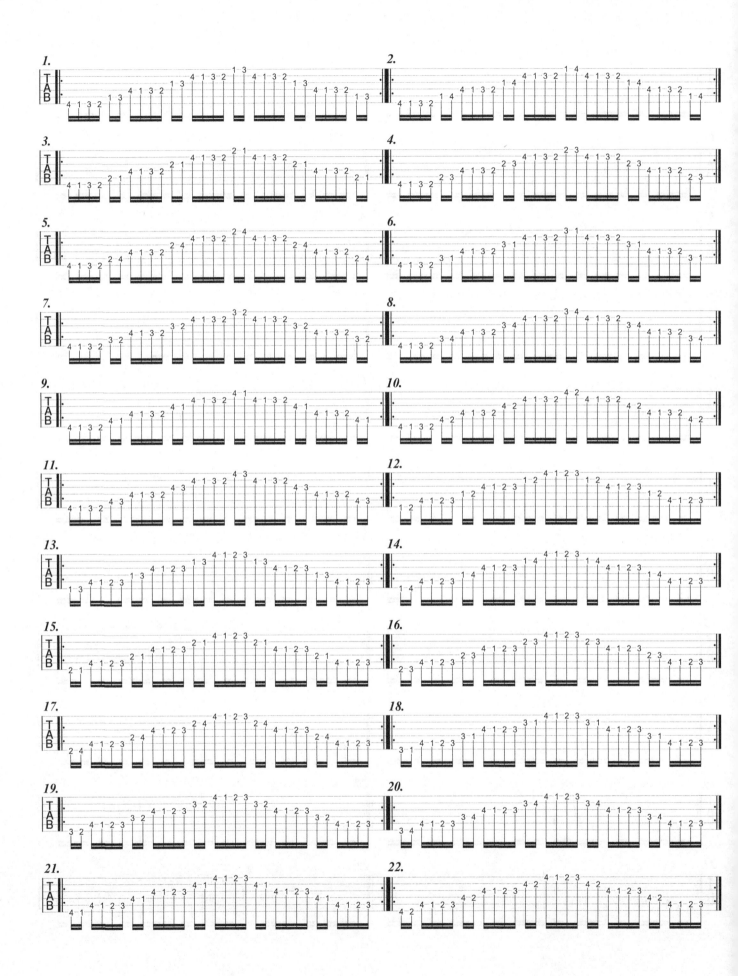

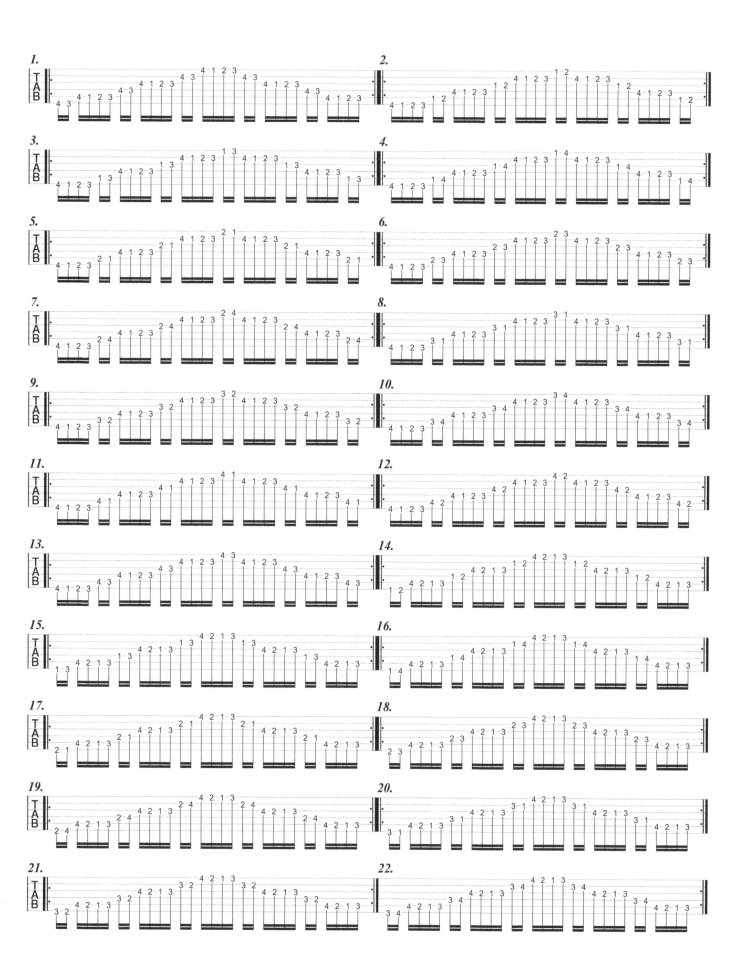

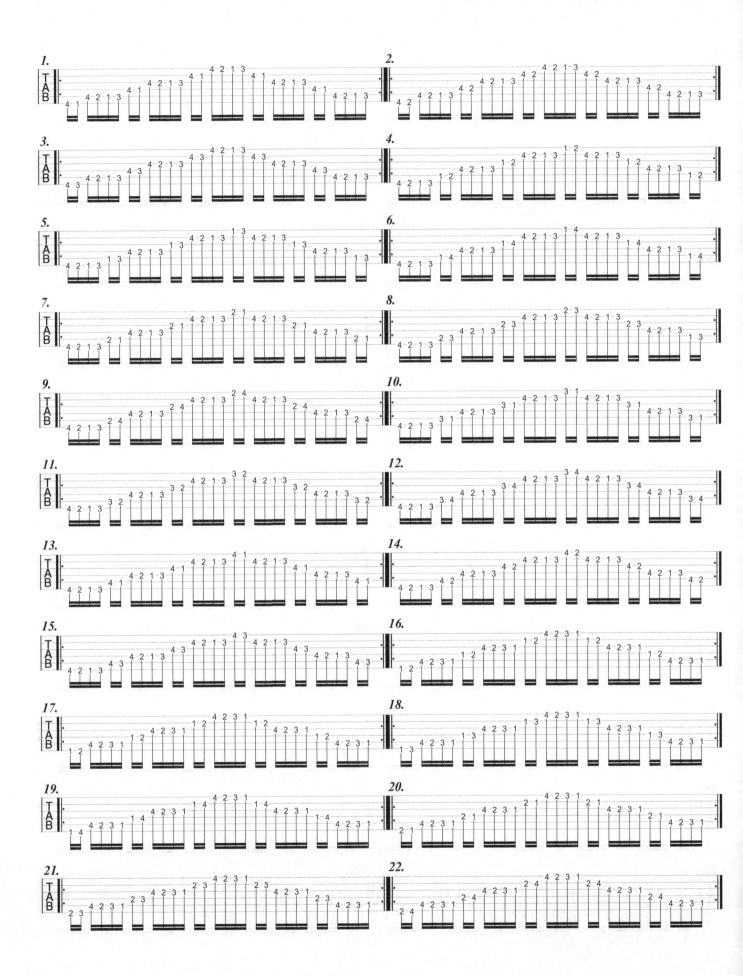

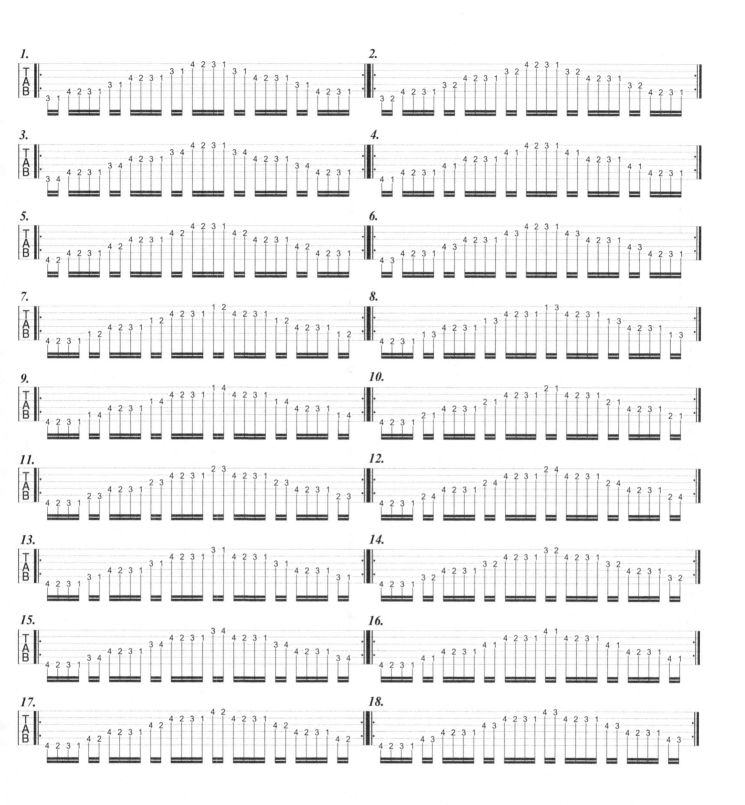

⇒ *Tip: You can apply 3 grouping or 4 grouping to any of the patterns in these sections.*

Three and Four Fingers

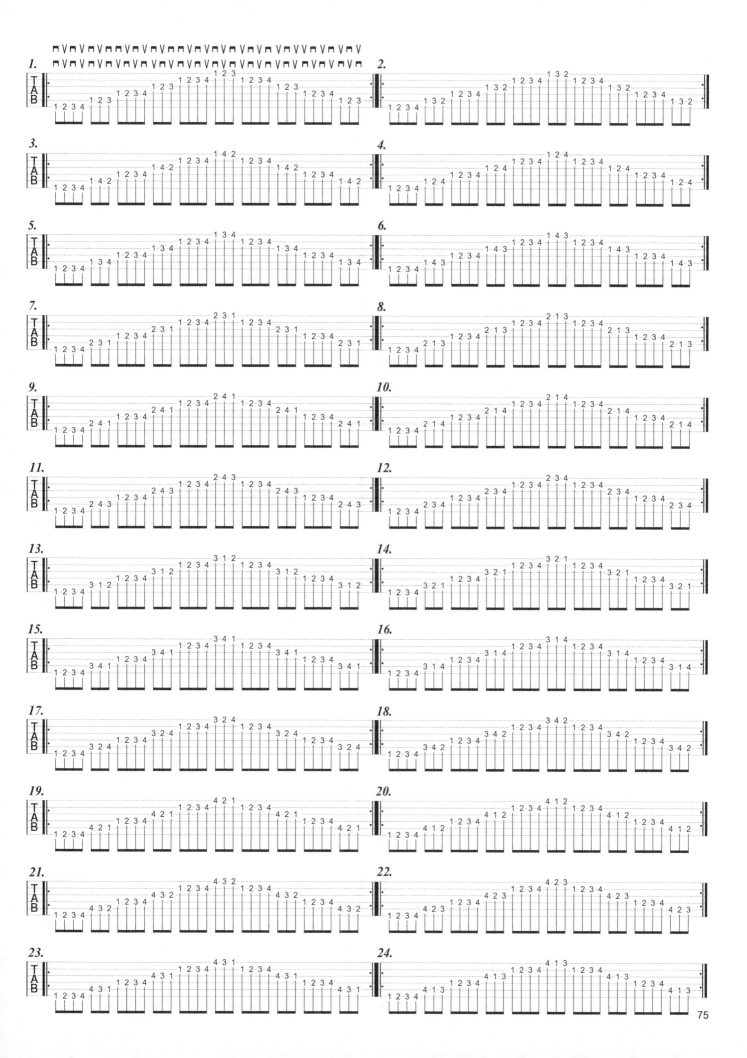

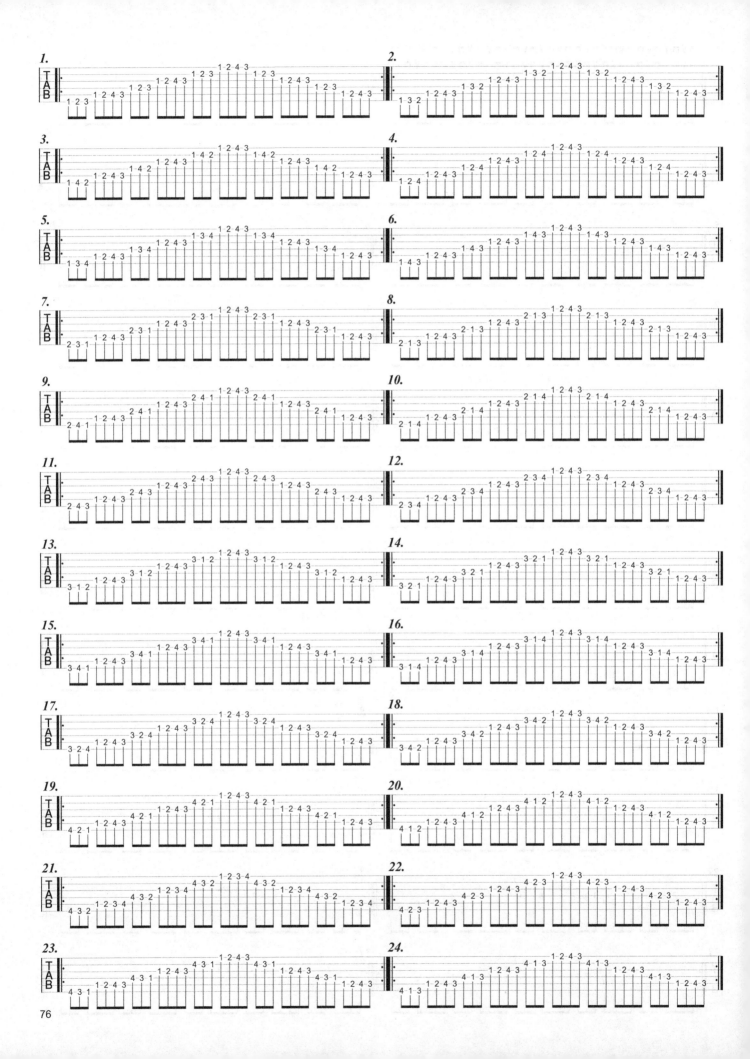

76

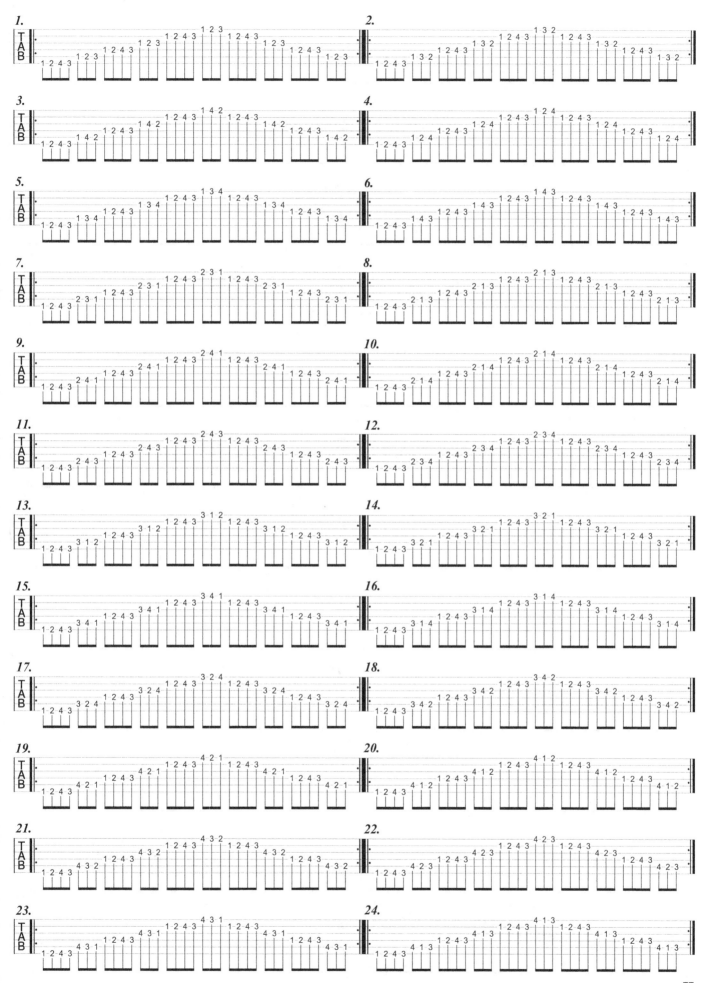

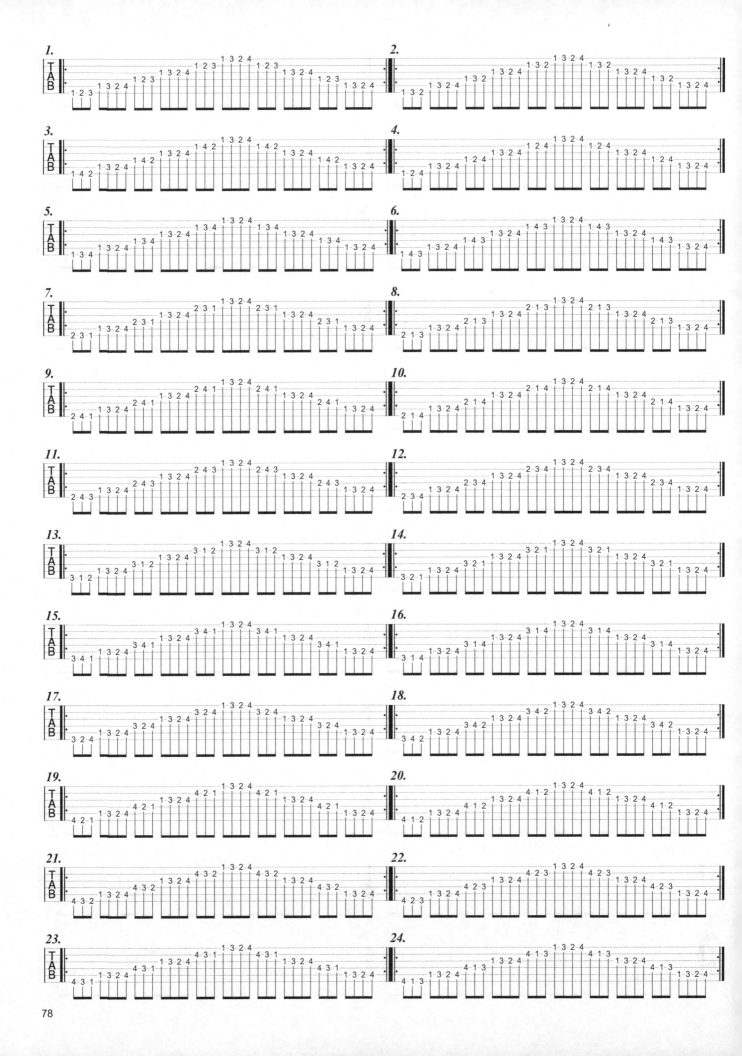

78

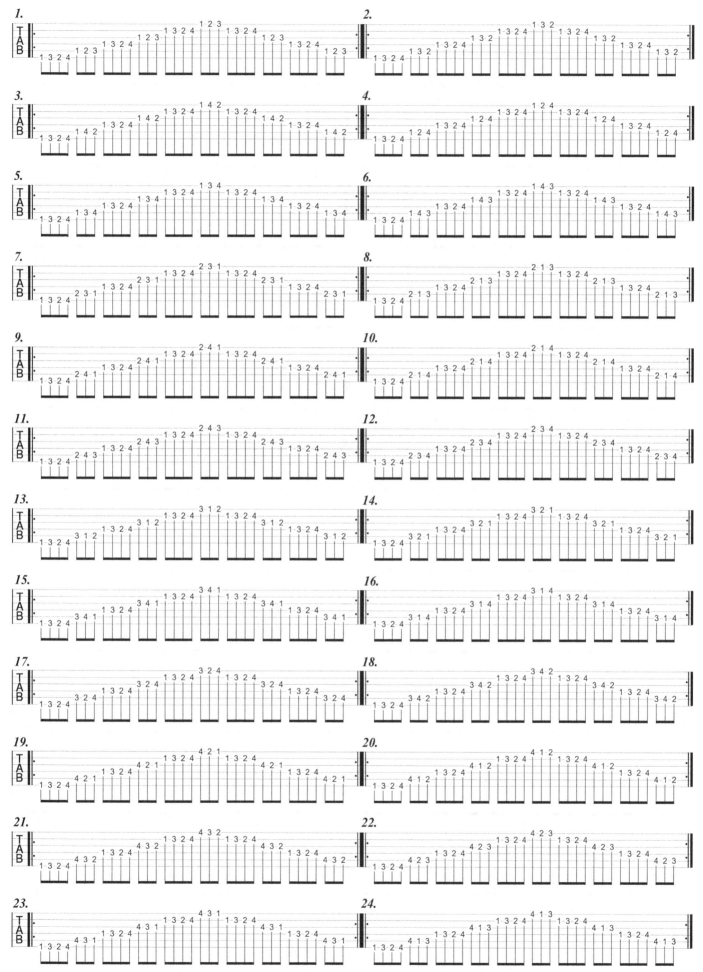

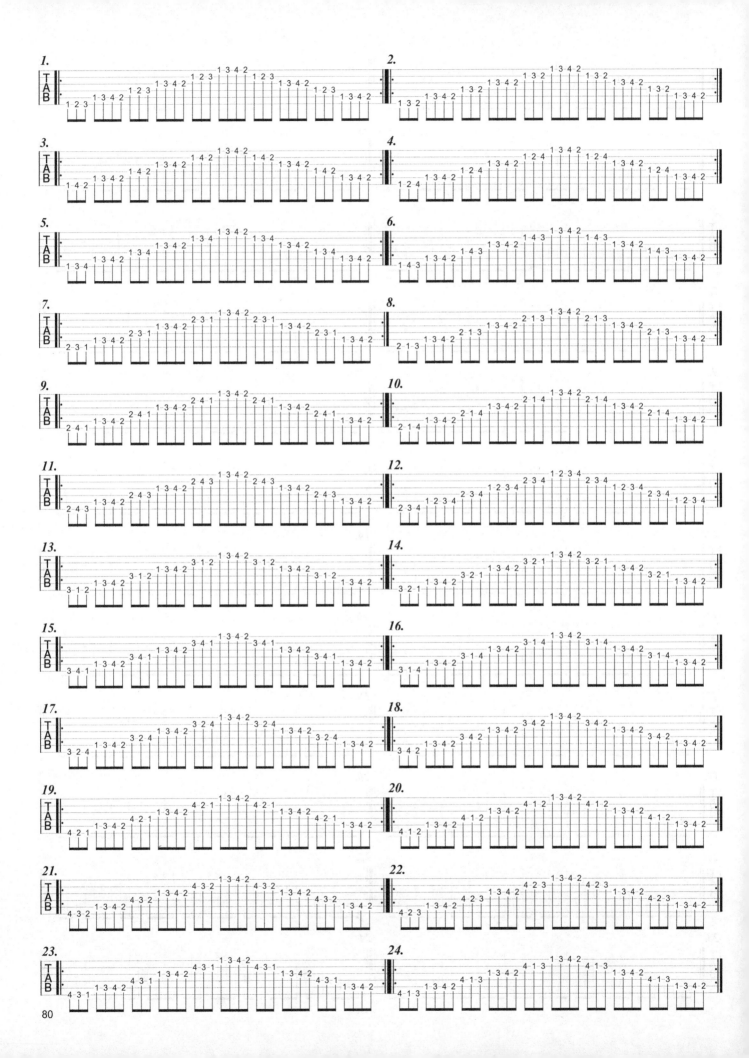

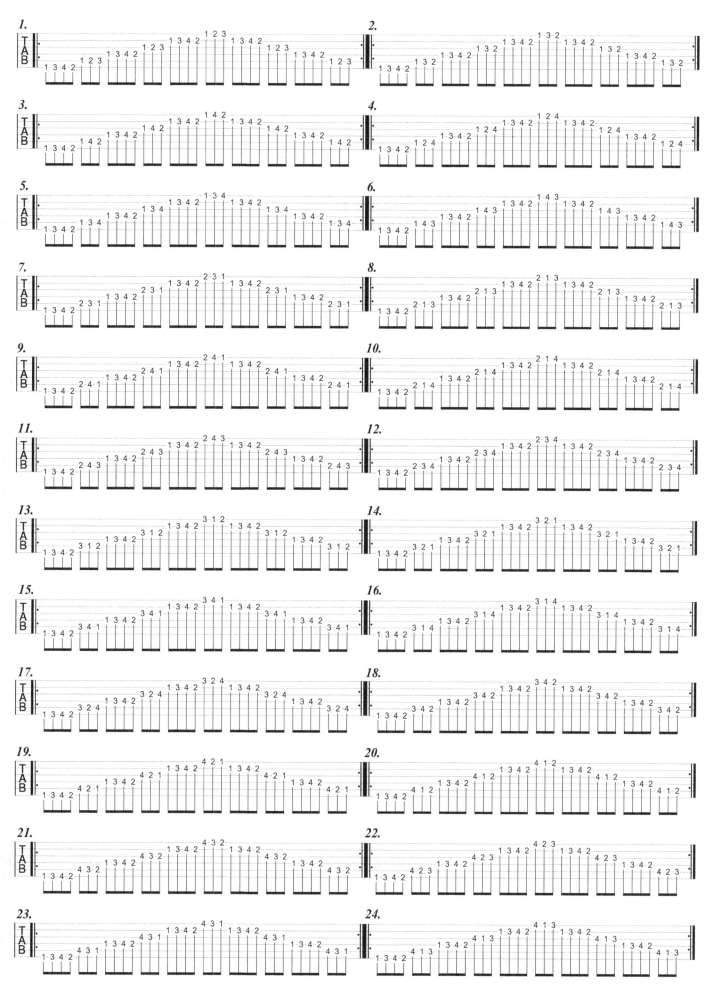

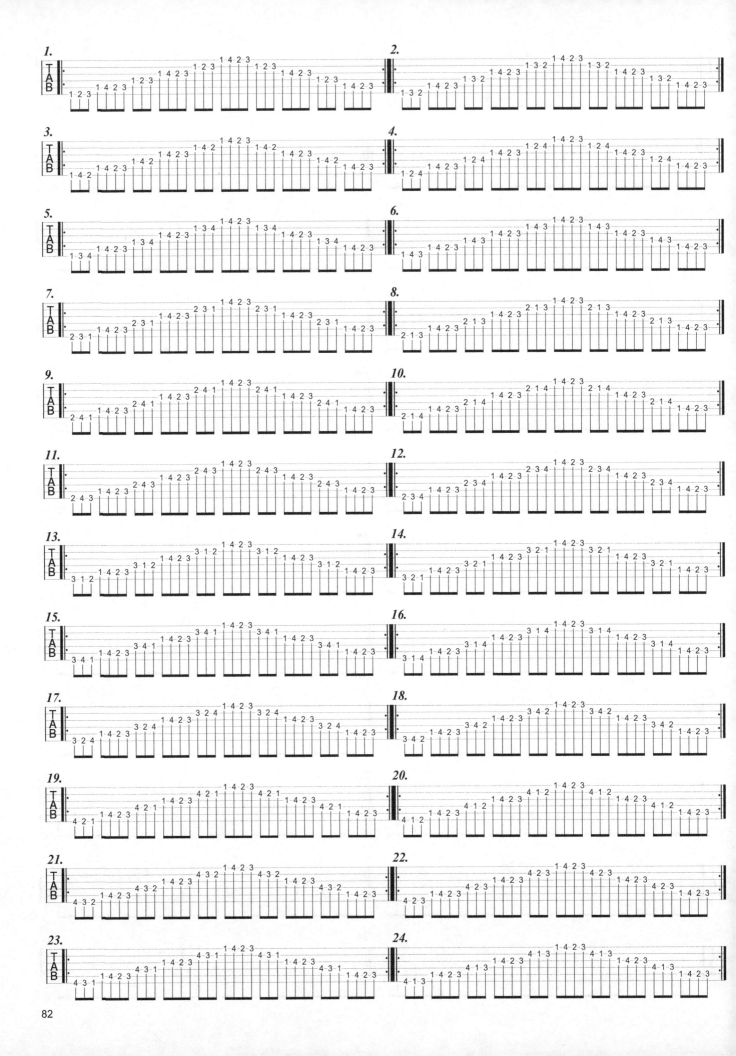

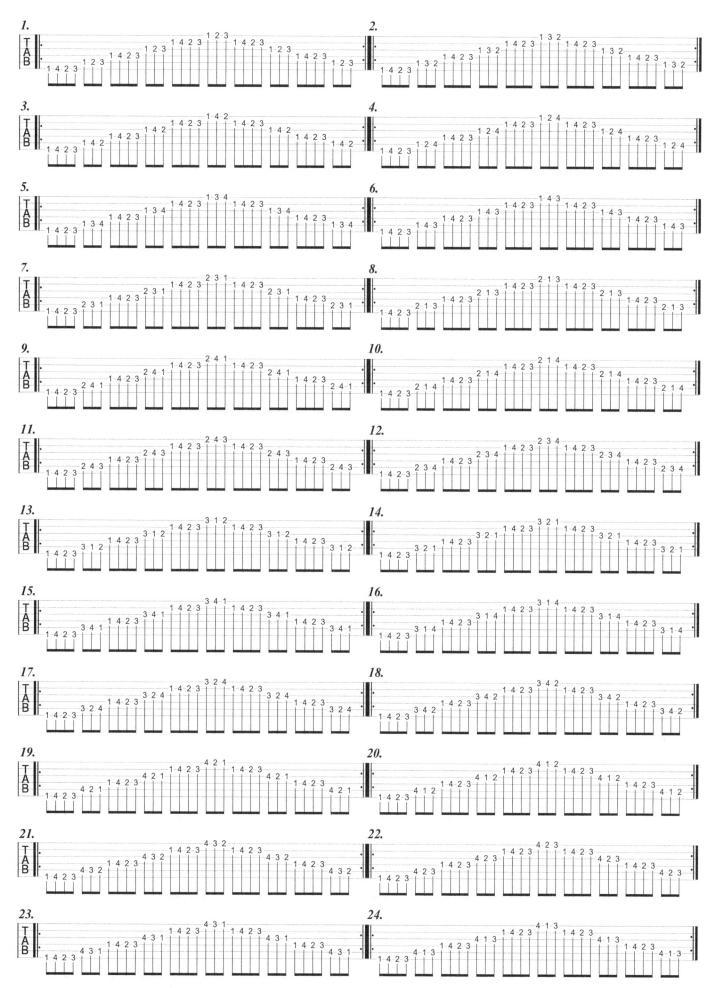

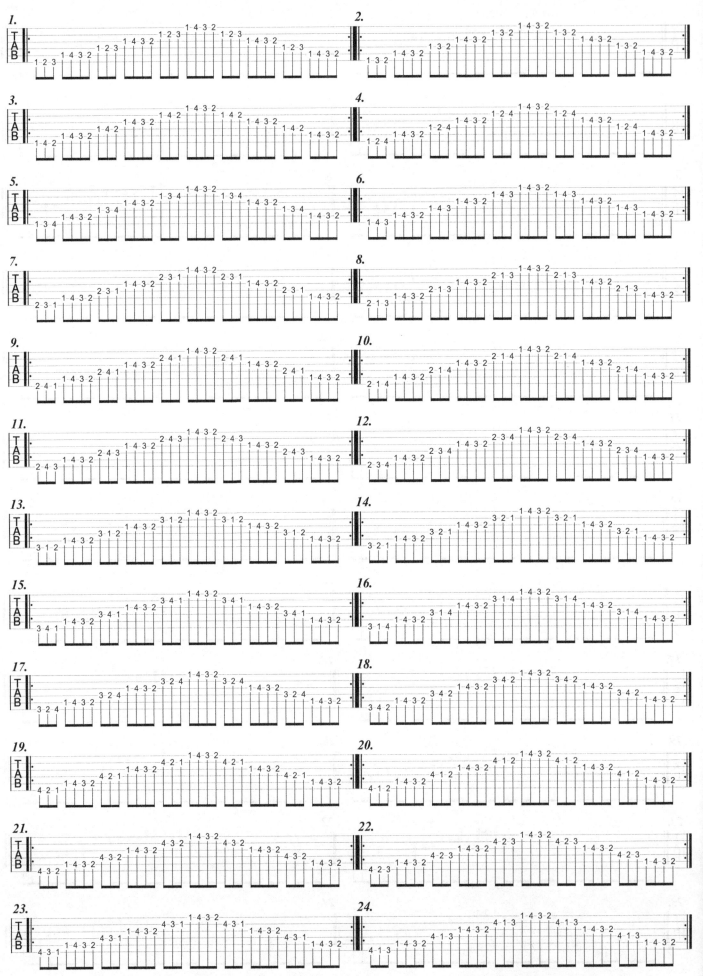

84

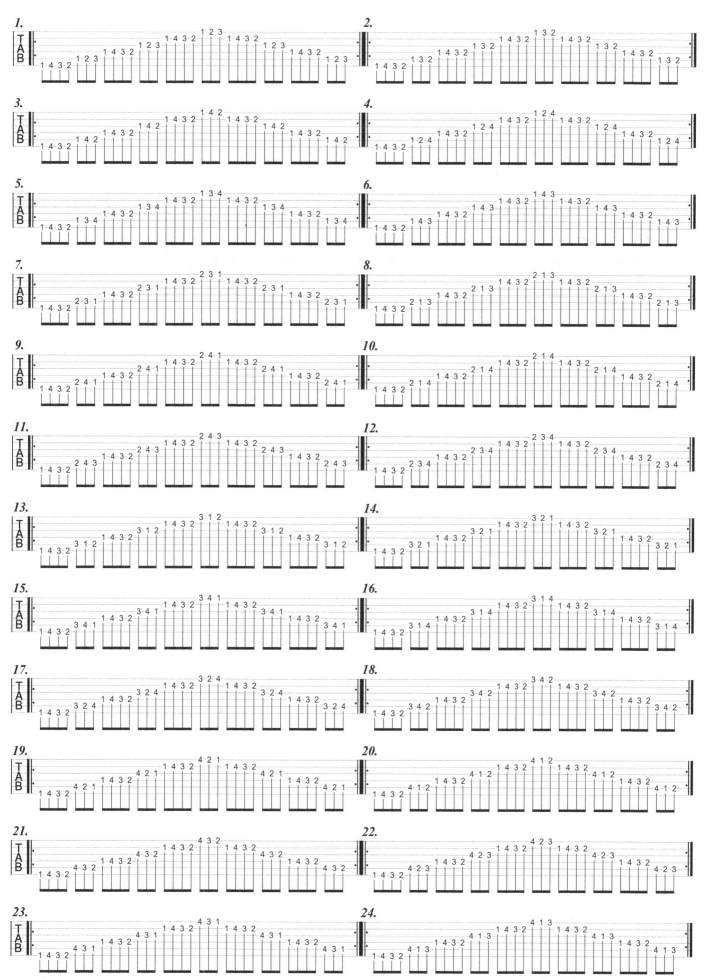

Between Two Strings

Between two strings: playing one note on a string to two notes on the next adjacent string or two notes on a string to one note on an adjacent string (similar to *spider walks*). These combinations are excellent for developing inside or outside picking techniques. They also help with traversing the strings by working directly on switching to the next string.

If you are a jazz or blues player, you can also try "swinging" the rhythm, concentrating more on alternate picking.

All of the examples are shown using alternate picking. The examples may be replayed using economy picking.

Economy picking patterns are shown on examples 1 and 3 to demonstrate how to apply economy picking to other exercises in this section.

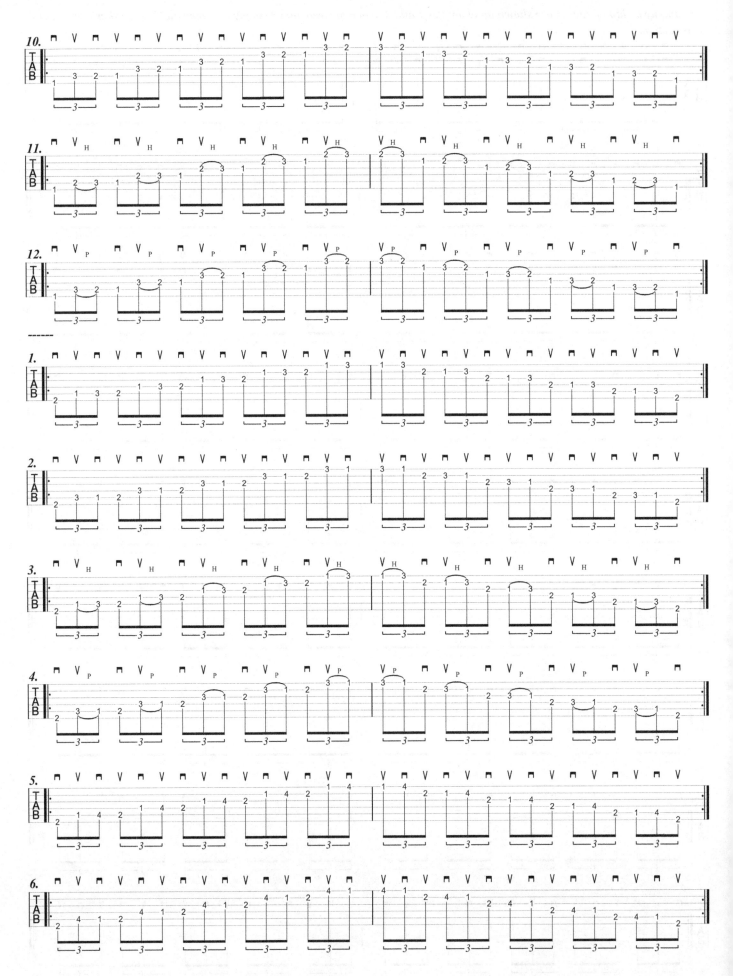

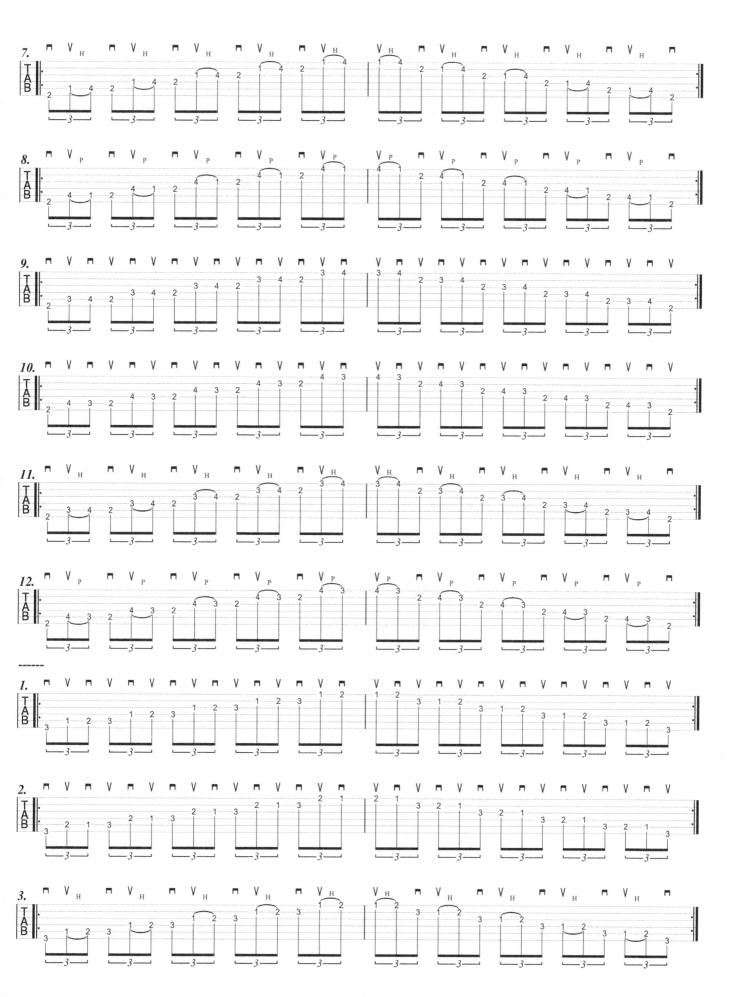

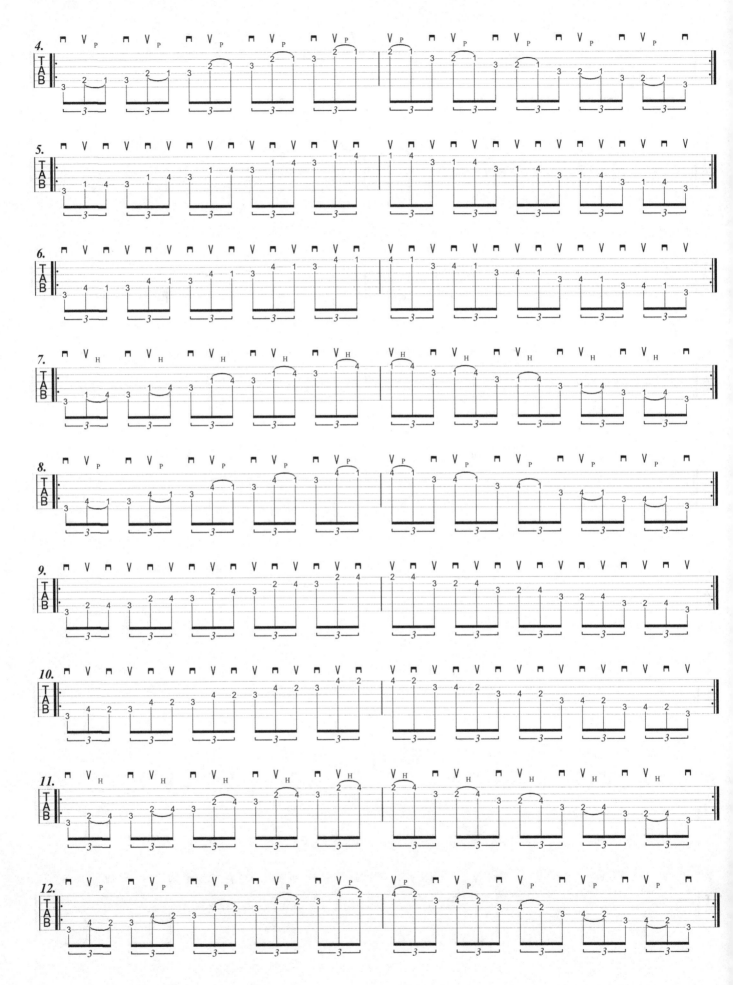

90

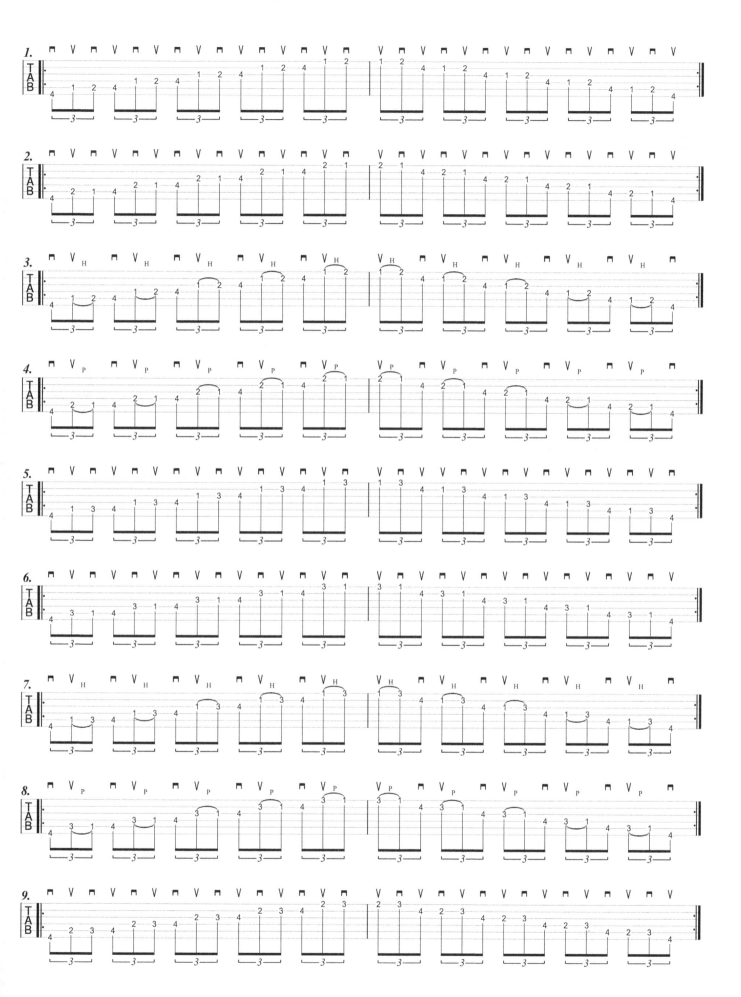

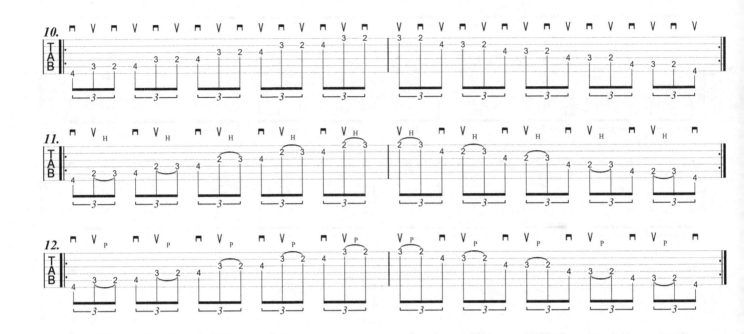

Between Two Strings 2

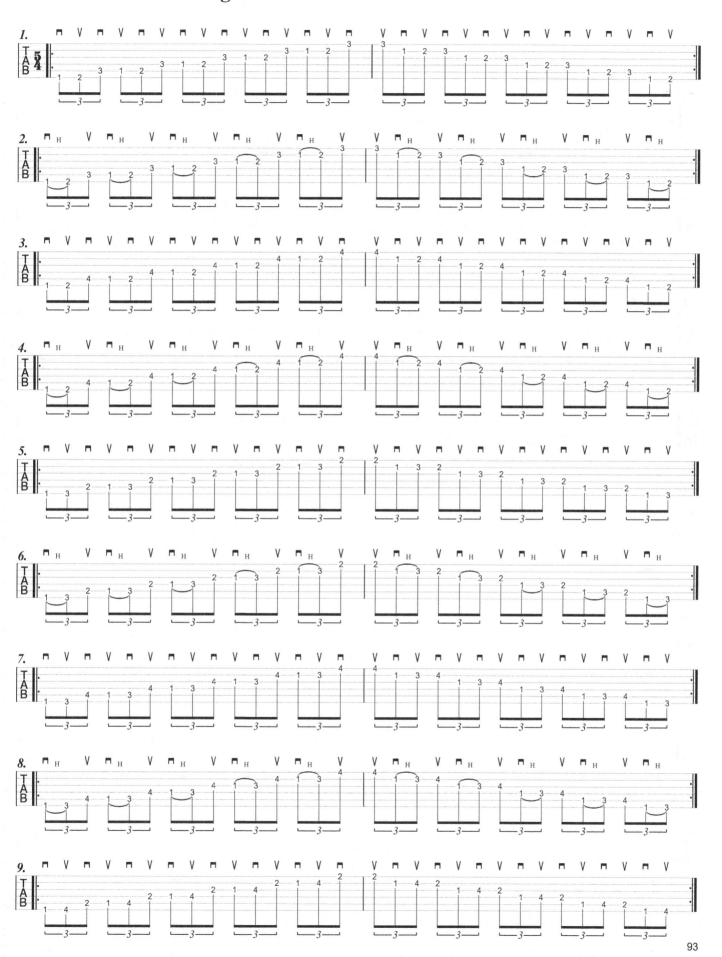

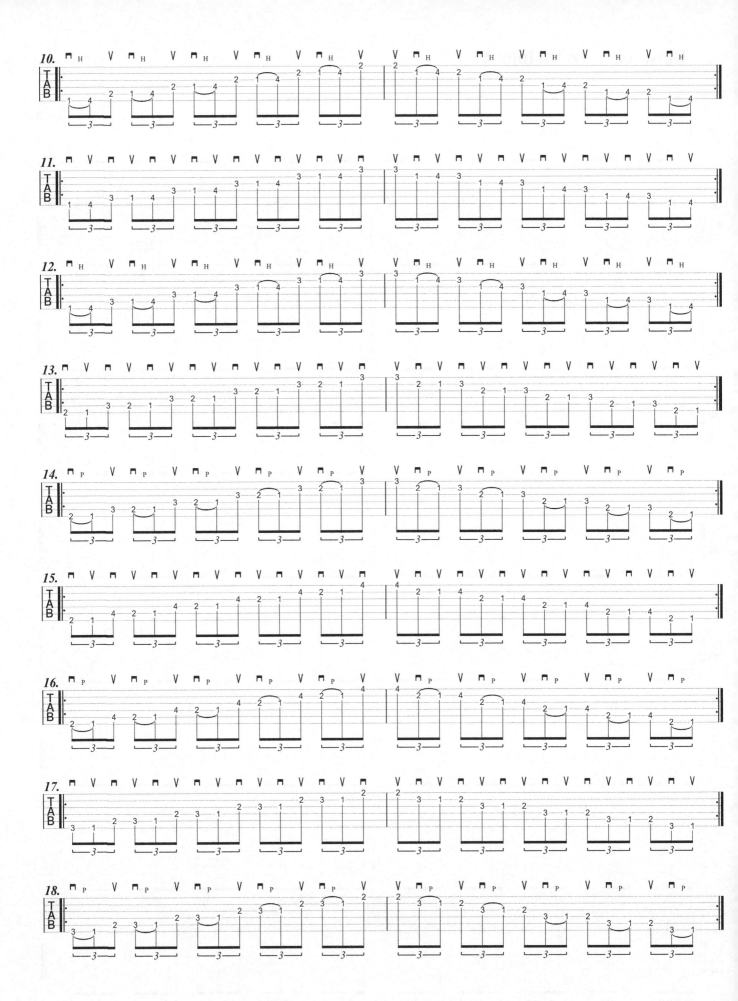

94

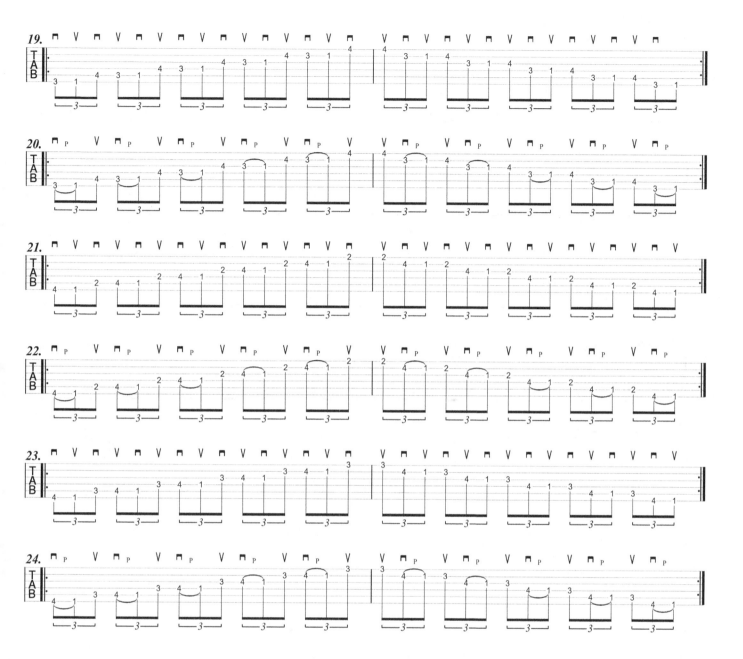

Turning Around

Quickly switching between ascending and descending.

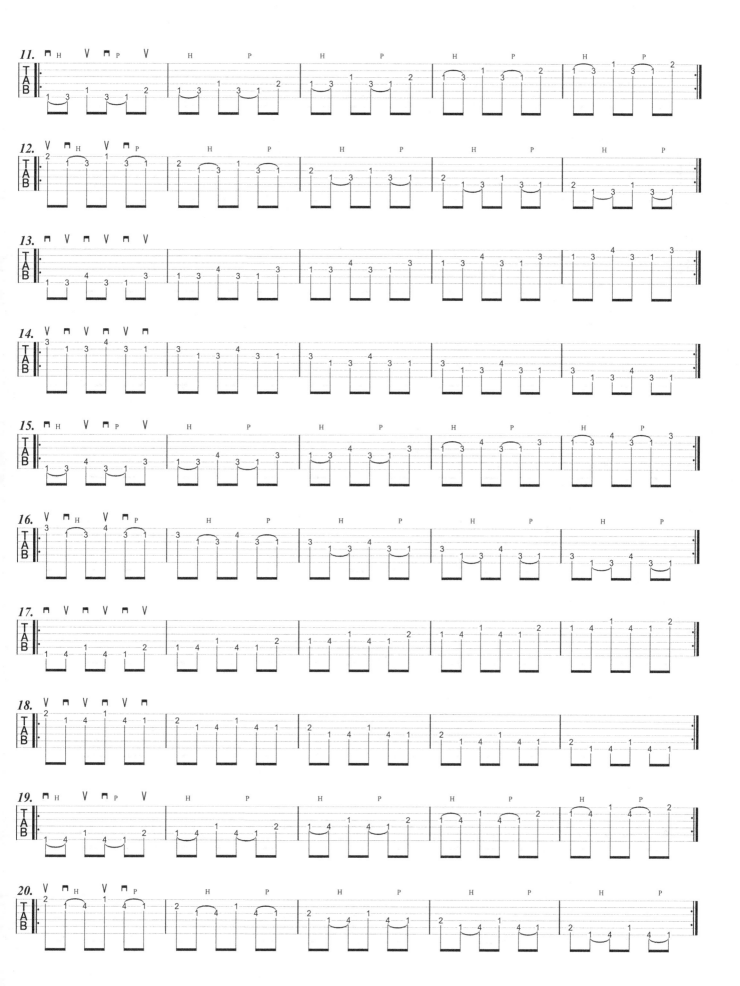

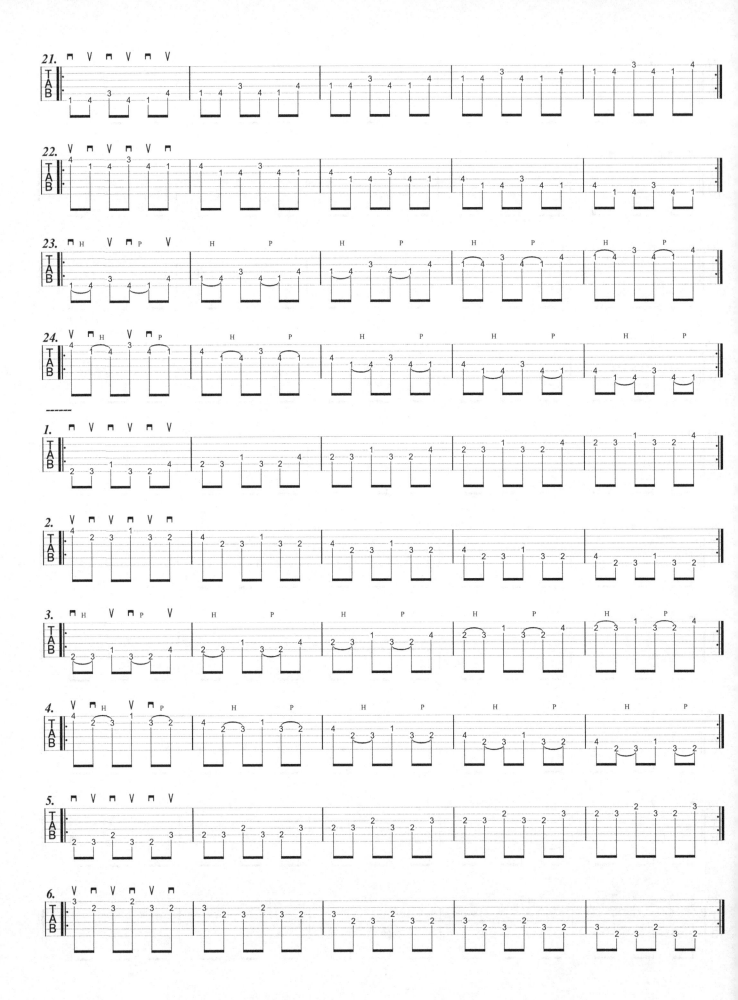

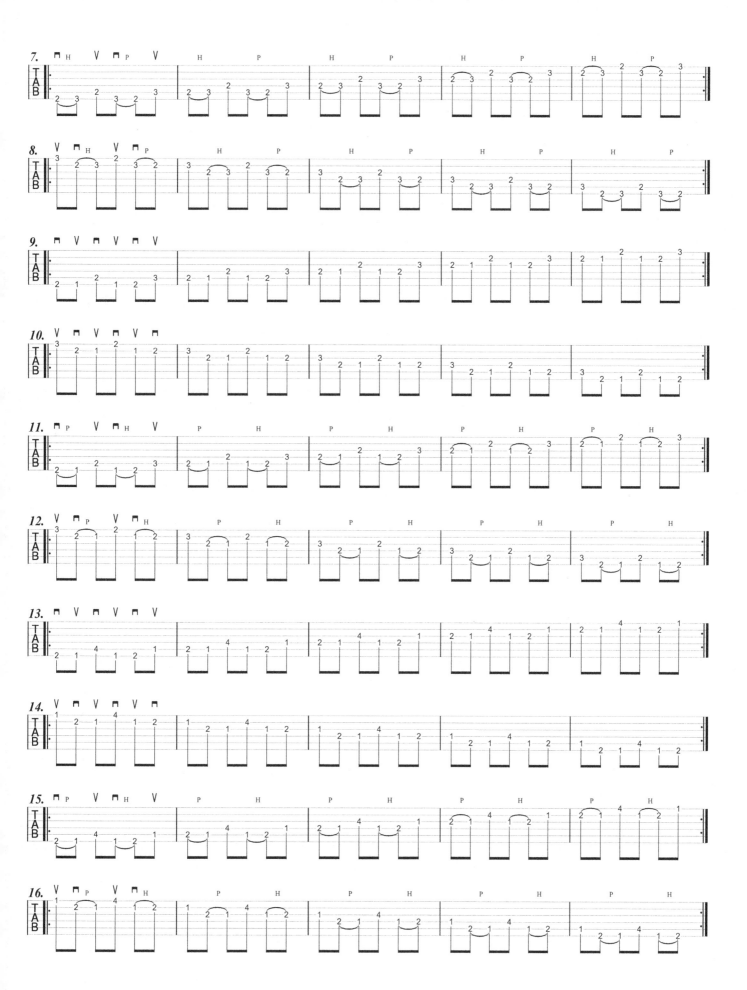

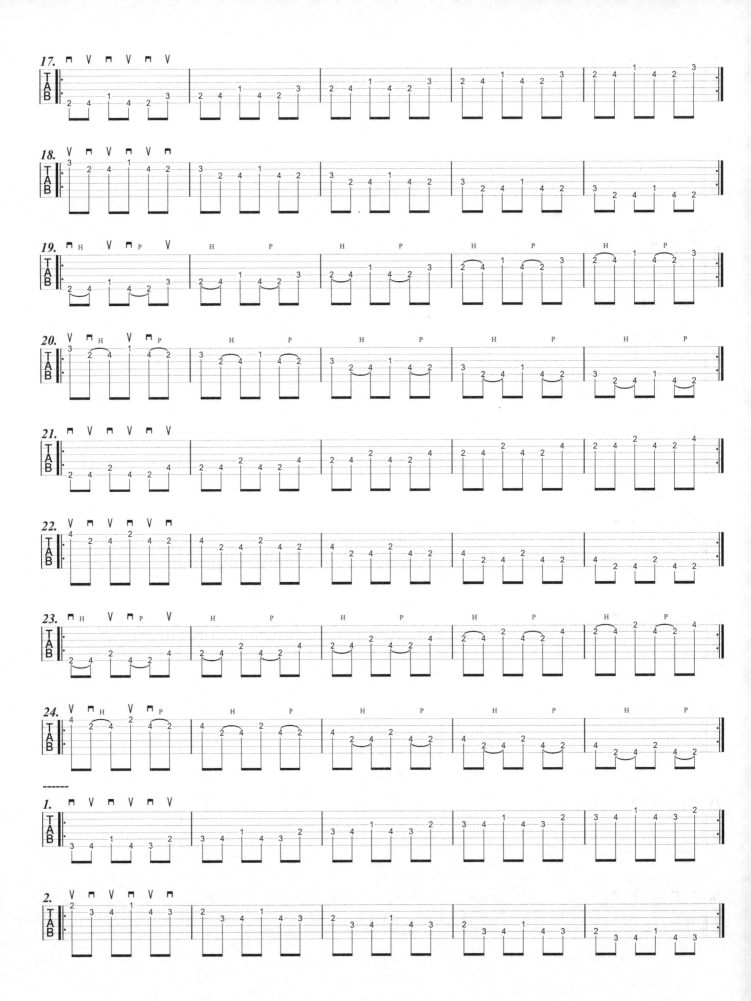

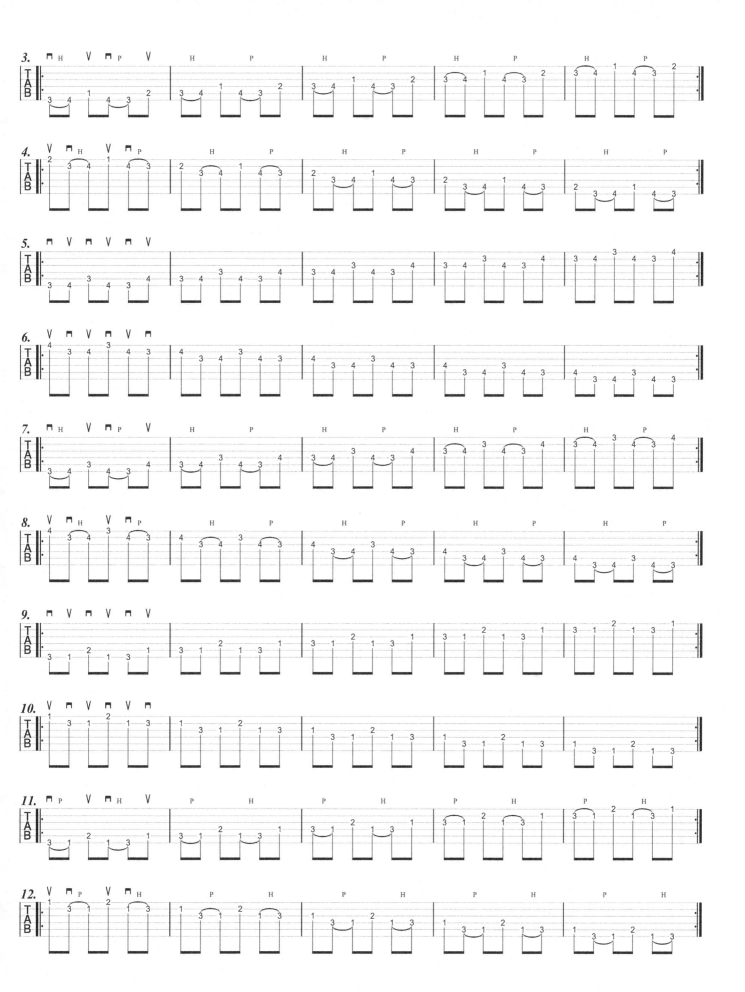

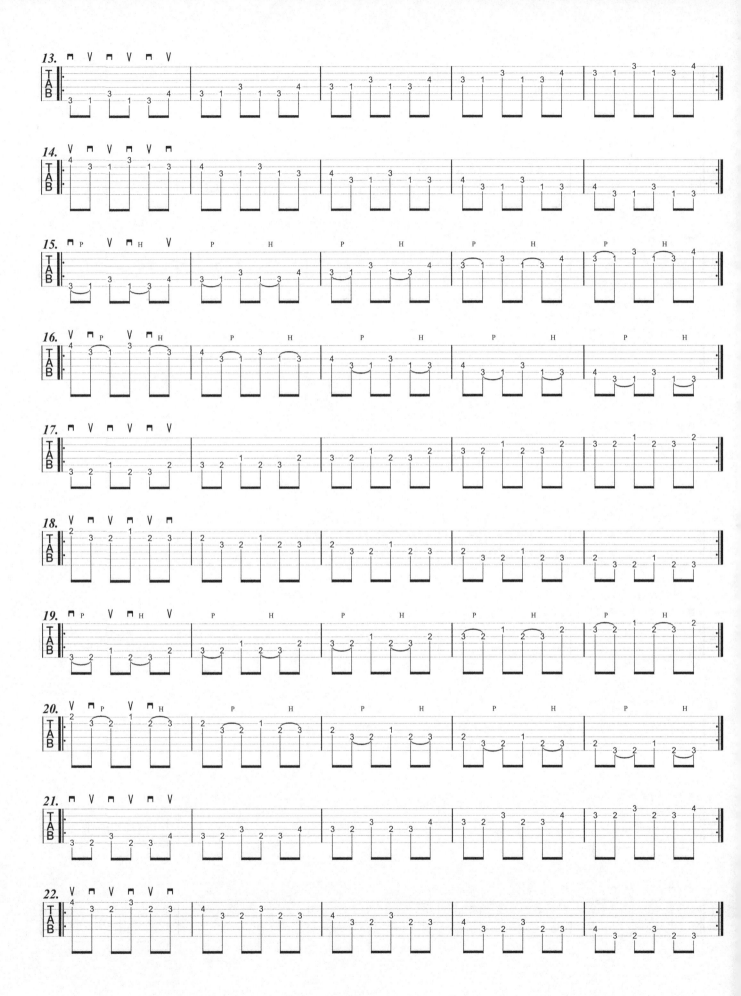

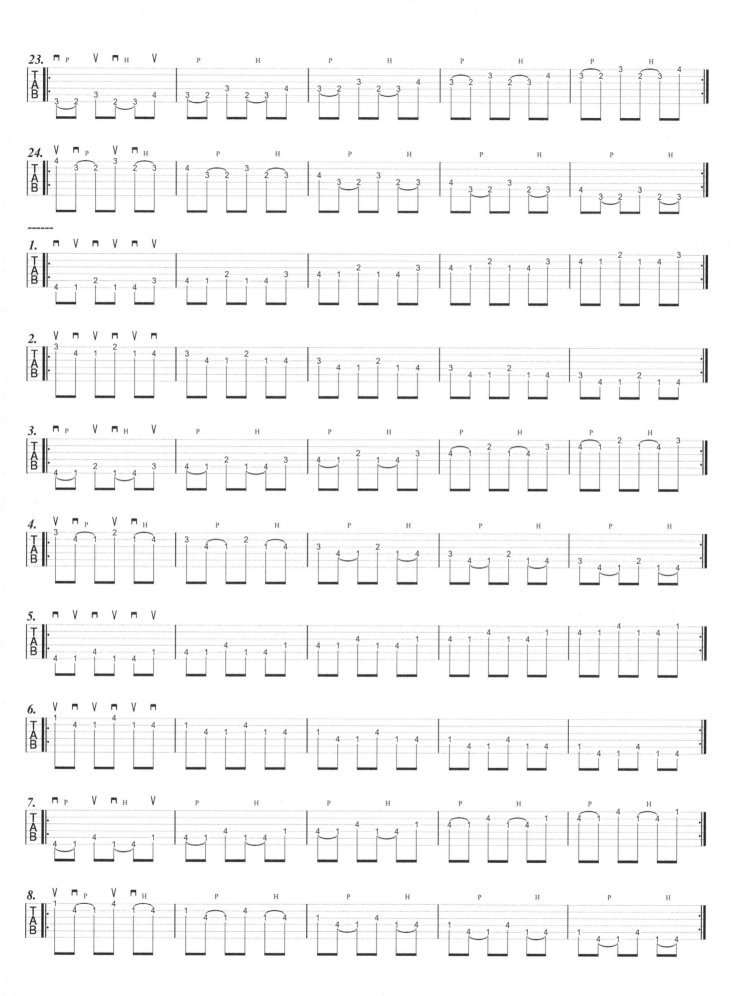

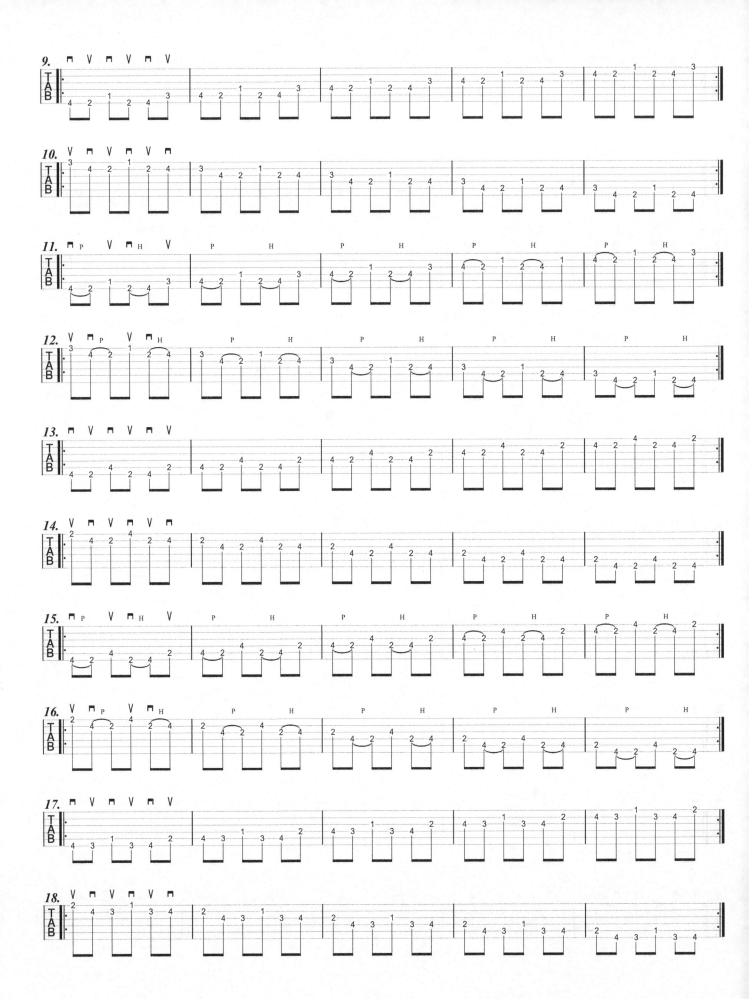

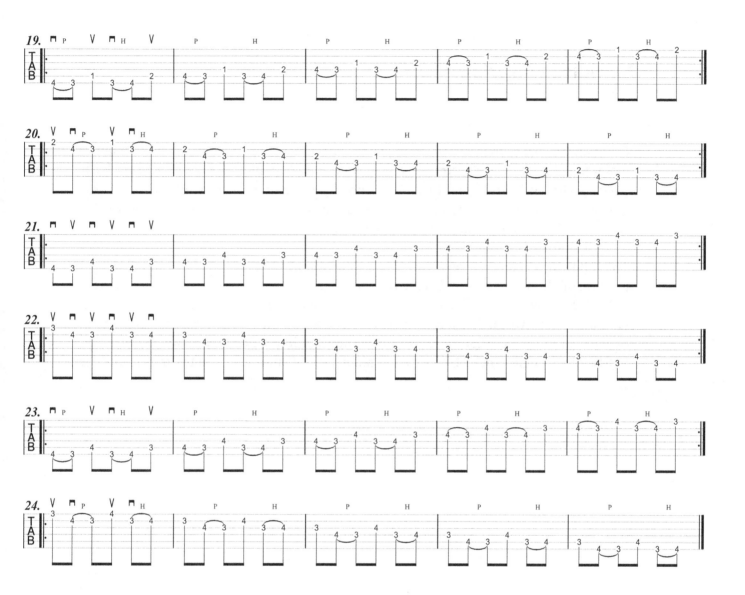

Extended Fingering

Curl your fingers as they would while playing the guitar. Notice the finger tips coming closer together? Now try to stretch your fingers, and you will notice the finger tips don't stretch apart much while your fingers are curled. Reaching for notes while your hand is *flattened* works because the fingers are not curled. The idea here is to strengthen your fingers so they can maintain a natural stretch while playing.

The following exercises extend your fingers one fret beyond the normal hand/finger position of all four fingers, in line, with each finger on its own fret. For example, fingers 1-2 usually play on frets right next to each other. But for these exercises, fingers 1-2 will have a fret in between. These exercises are written from the 5th fret, which is a good overall starting place. Higher frets will be easier, and lower frets, especially the first fret, will be challenging. These exercises will build strength and control in the fret-hand fingers.

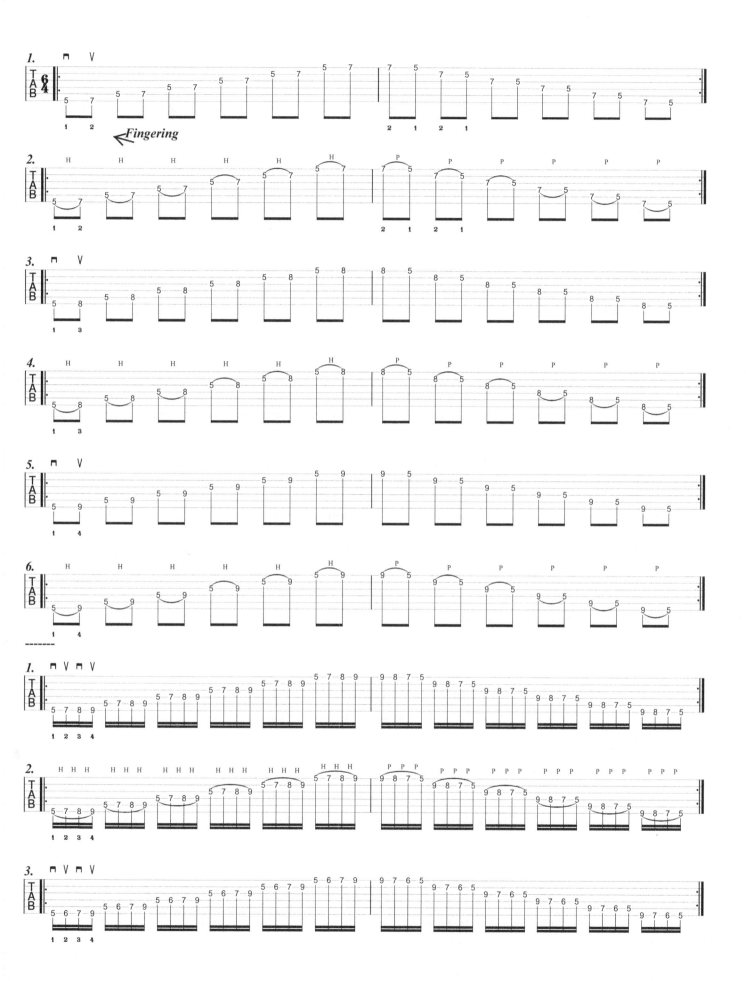

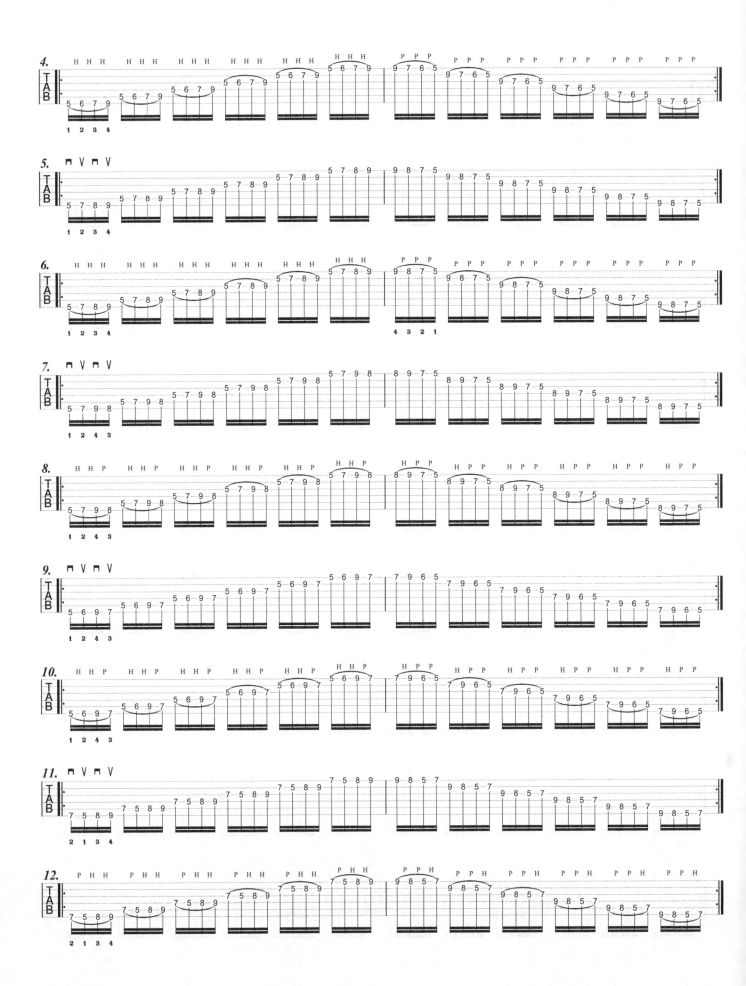

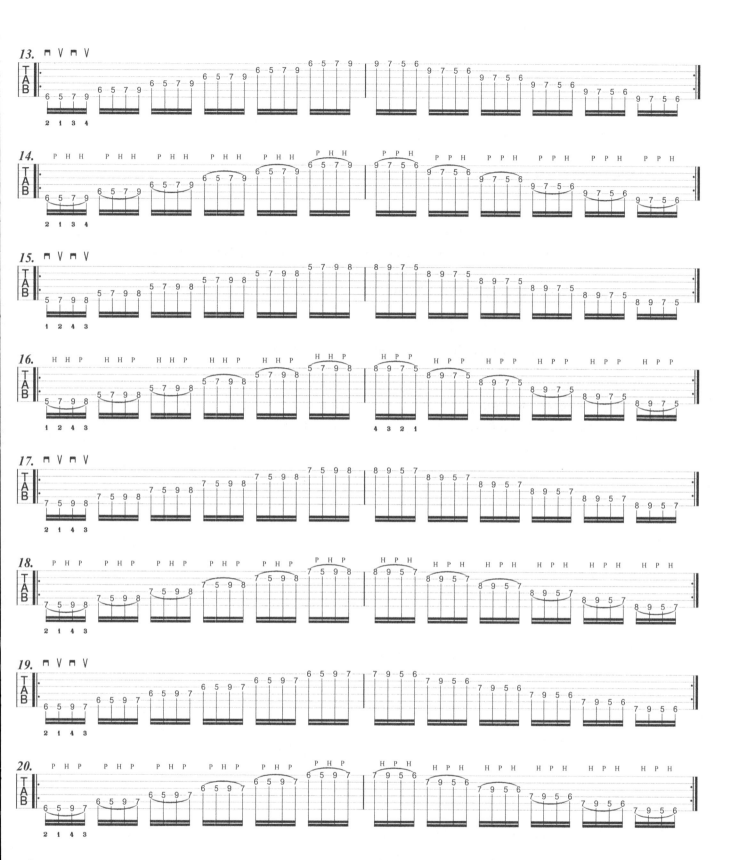

Linear Exercises

These exercises help with rapidly changing positions on the guitar. Your hand will shift into different positions, and your fingers, including your thumb, should use light pressure. Your thumb should move with your hand to avoid dragging your thumb.

These exercises are great for gaining picking speed while making quick position changes up and down the neck.

Exercises will mix alternate picking, hammer-ons, and pull-offs in a different way, and large areas of the fretboard will be covered. fingers.

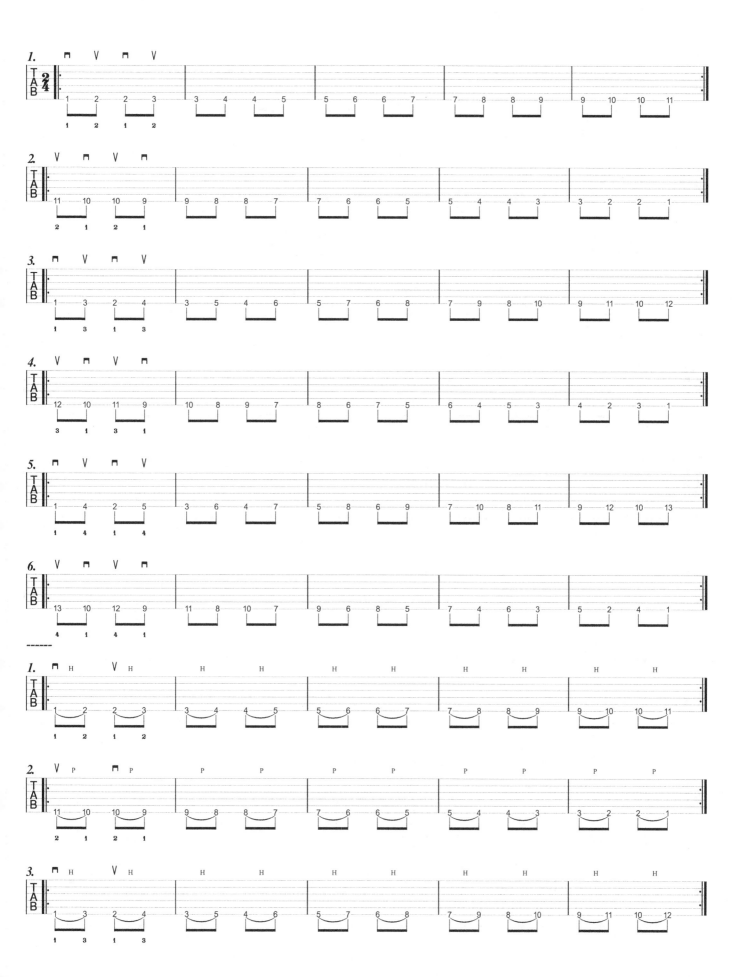

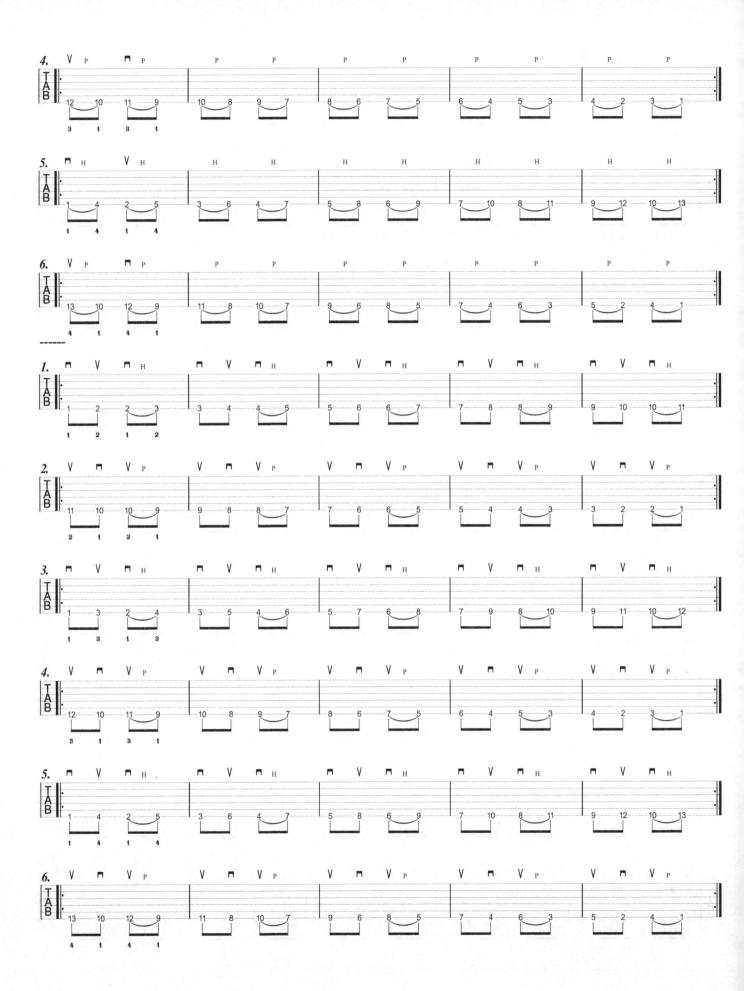

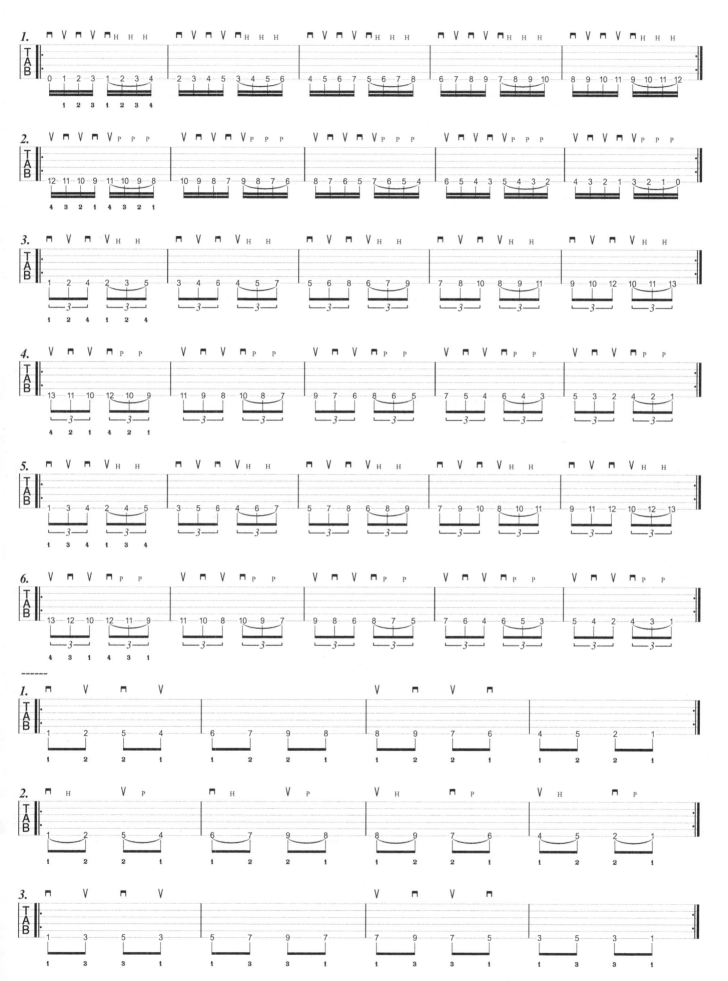

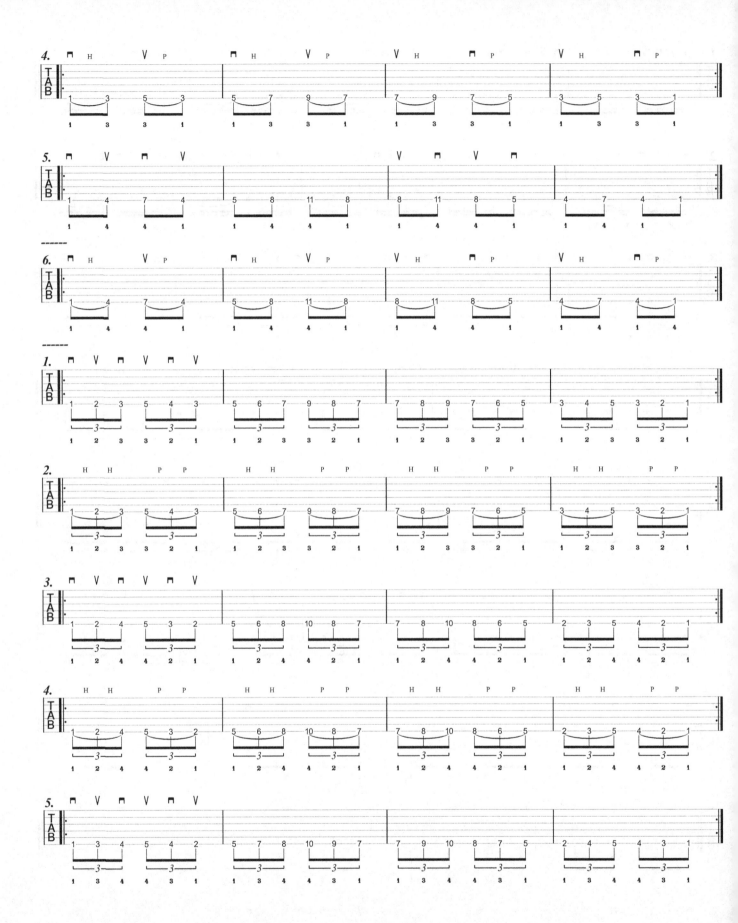

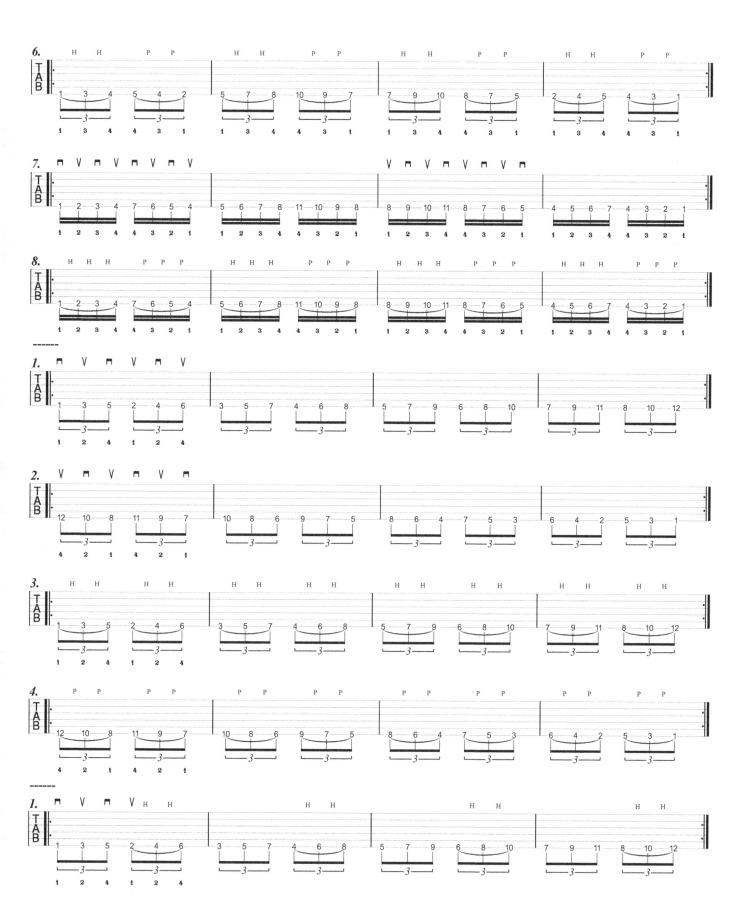

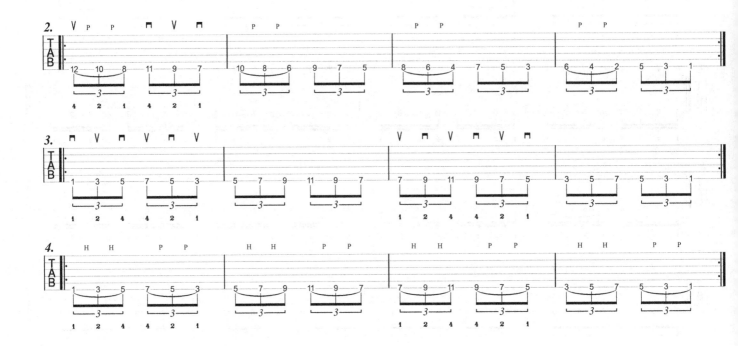

Pivoting 1

*Pivoting: returning to a note over and over. These endurance exercises will sound musical.
Use alternate picking throughout.*

1. ∏ V ∏ V ∏ V ∏ V

1 2 1 3 1 2 1 4

2. V ∏ V ∏ V ∏ V ∏

4 1 2 1 3 1 2 1

3. ∏H V H ∏H V H

1 2 1 3 1 2 1 4

4. V P ∏ P V P ∏ P

4 1 2 1 3 1 2 1

5. ∏ V ∏ V ∏ V ∏ V

1 3 1 2 1 3 1 4

6. V ∏ V ∏ V ∏ V ∏

4 1 3 1 2 1 3 1

7. ∏H V H ∏H V H

1 3 1 2 1 3 1 4

8. V P ∏ P V P ∏ P

4 1 3 1 2 1 3 1

9. ∏ V ∏ V ∏ V ∏ V

1 4 1 2 1 4 1 3

10. V ∏ V ∏ V ∏ V ∏

3 1 4 1 2 1 4 1

117

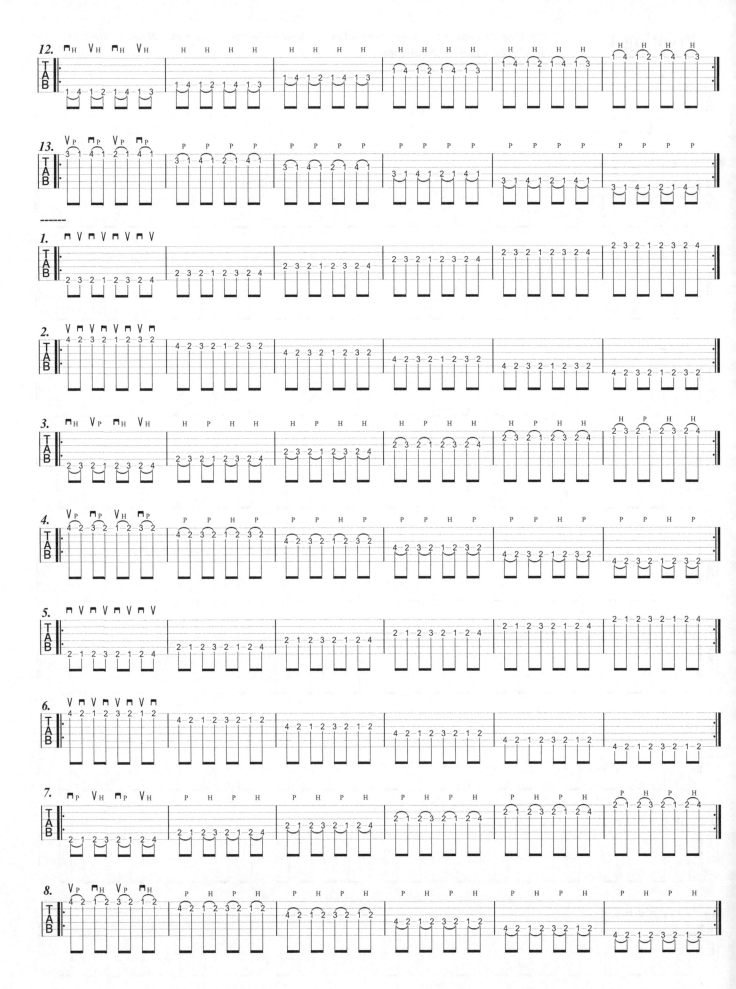

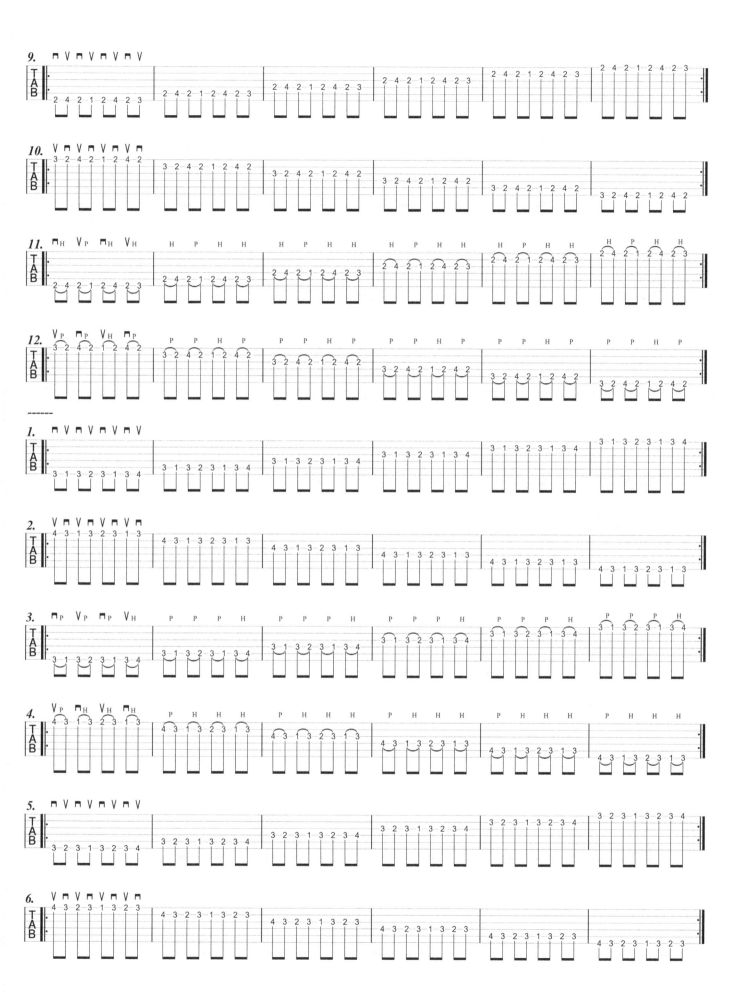

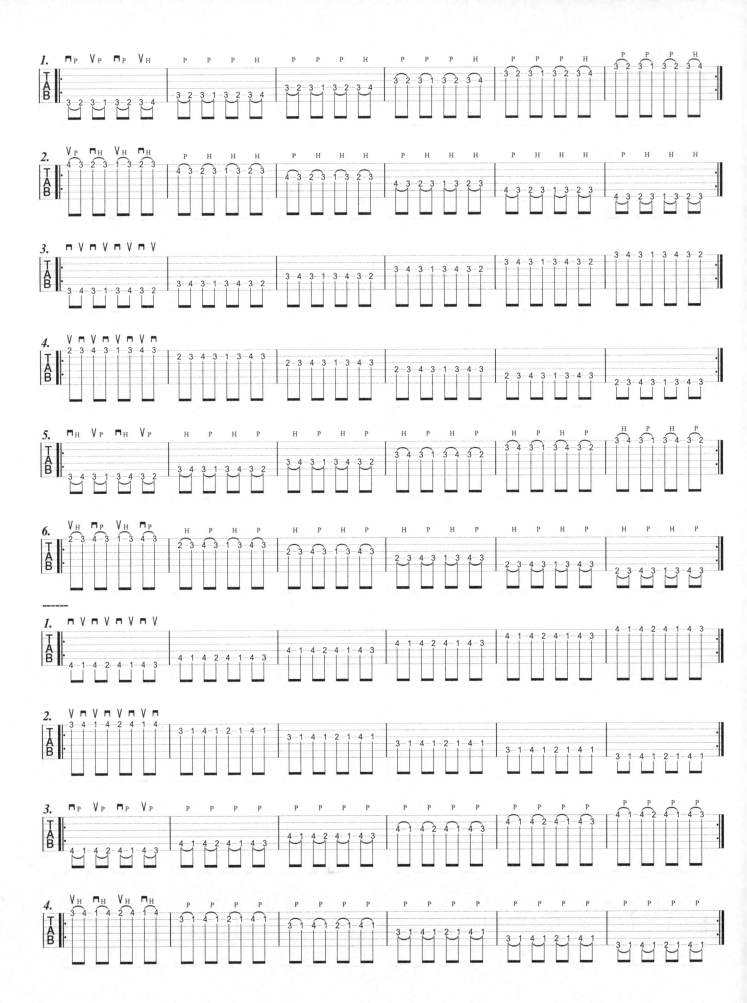

120

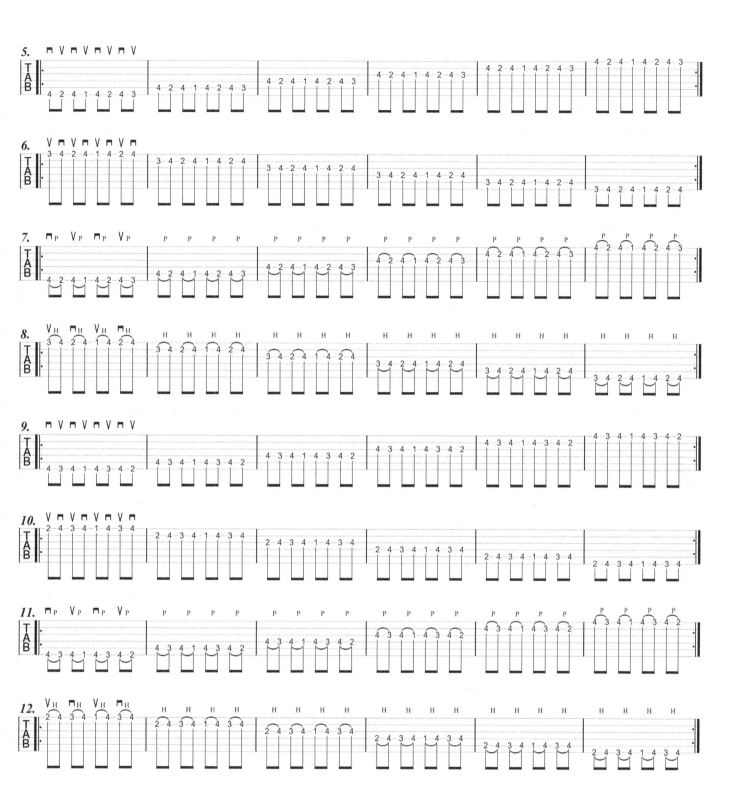

Pivoting 2

Reminder: picking can be reversed.

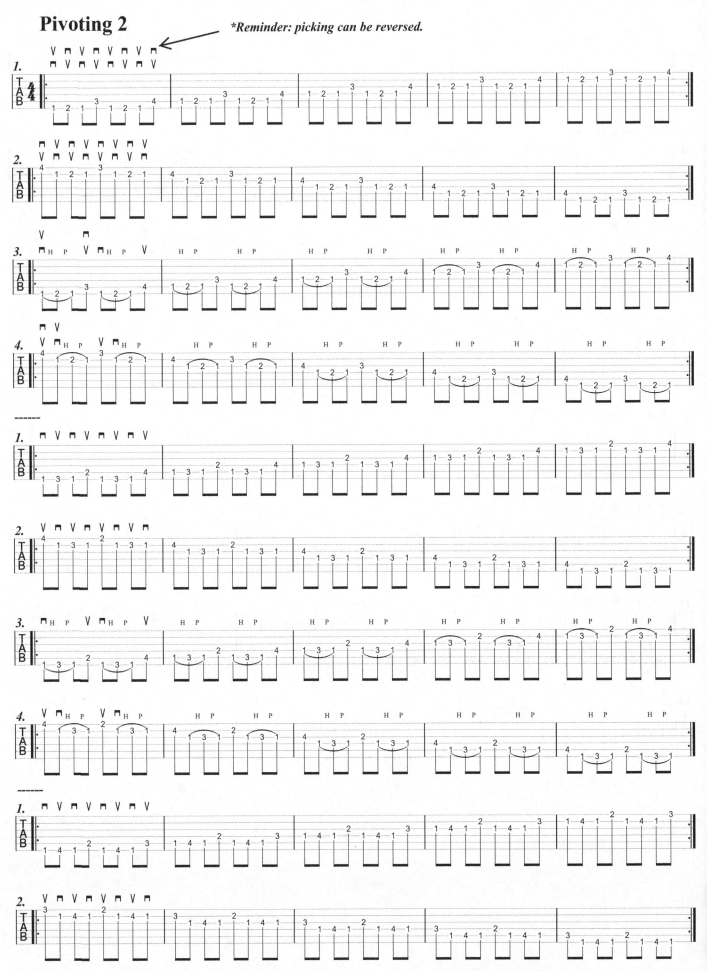

122

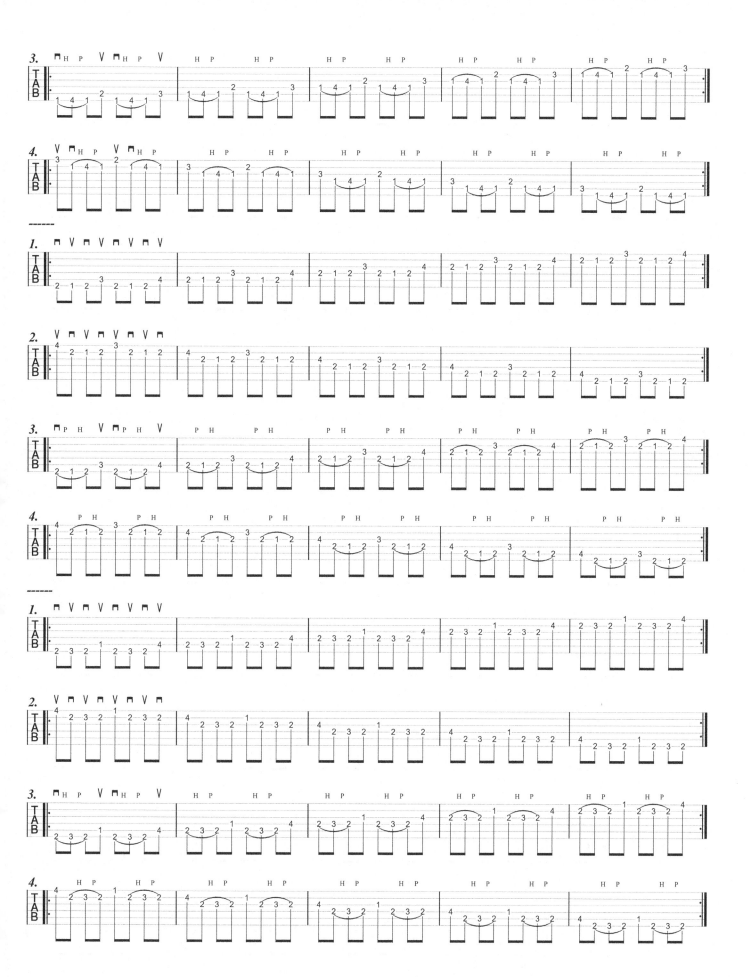

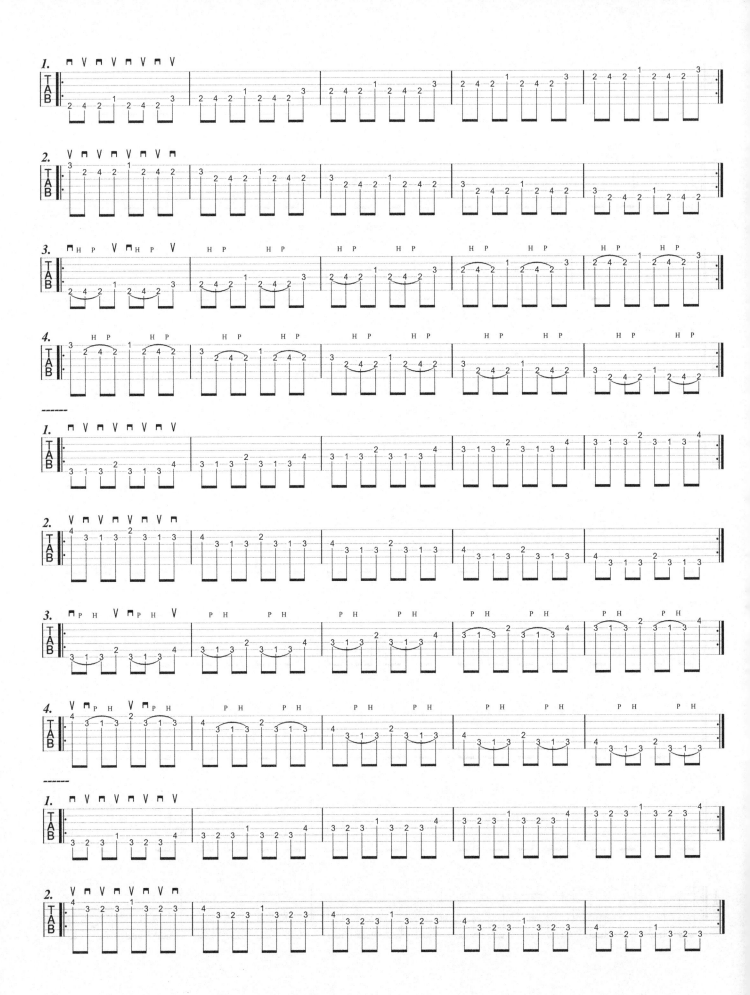

124

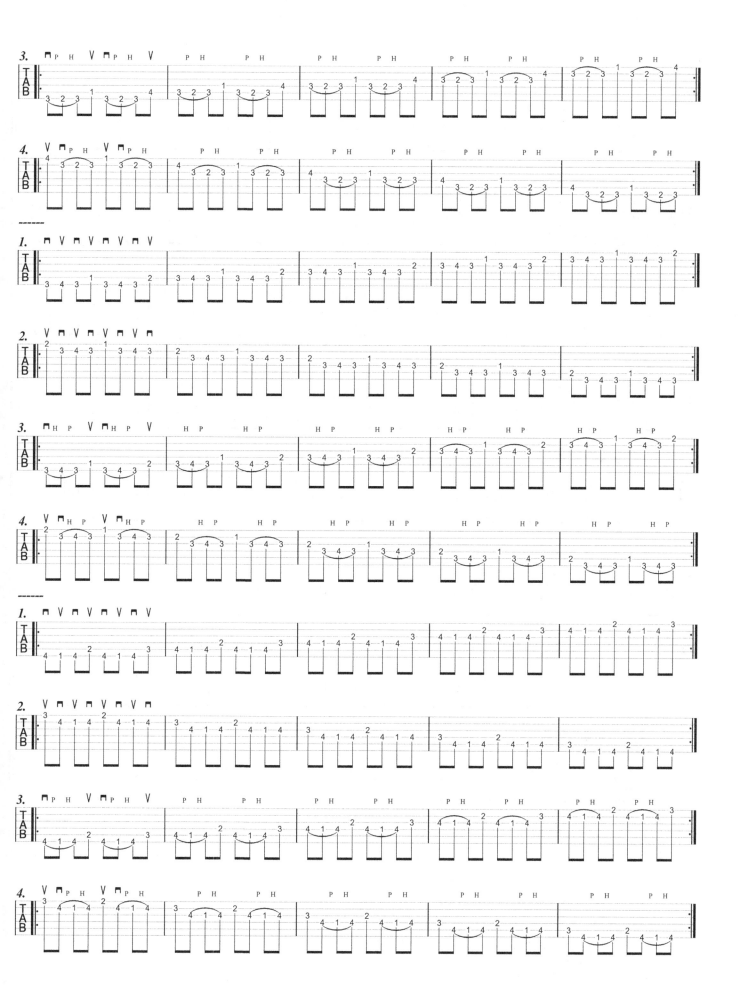

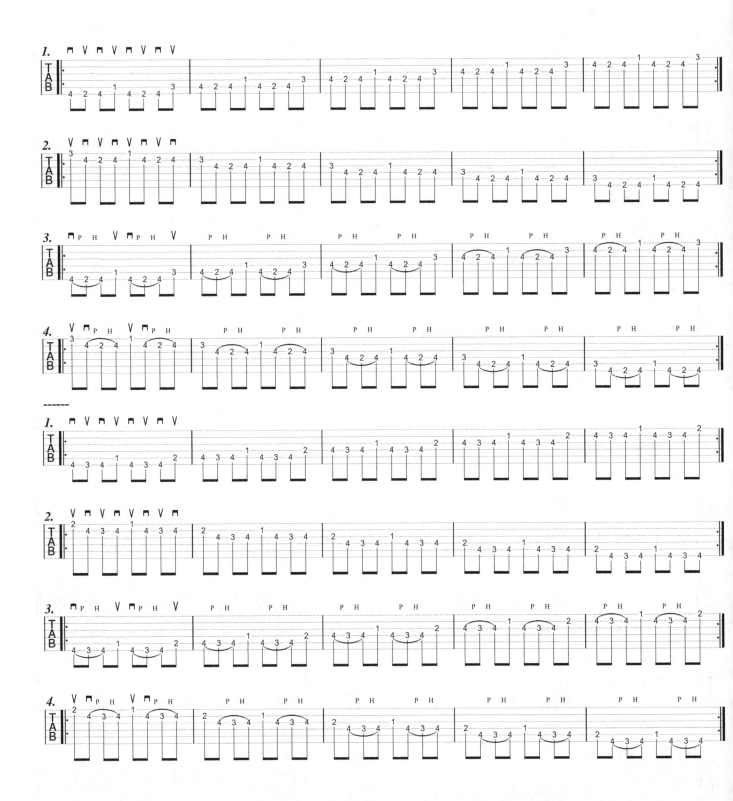

Return Fingering

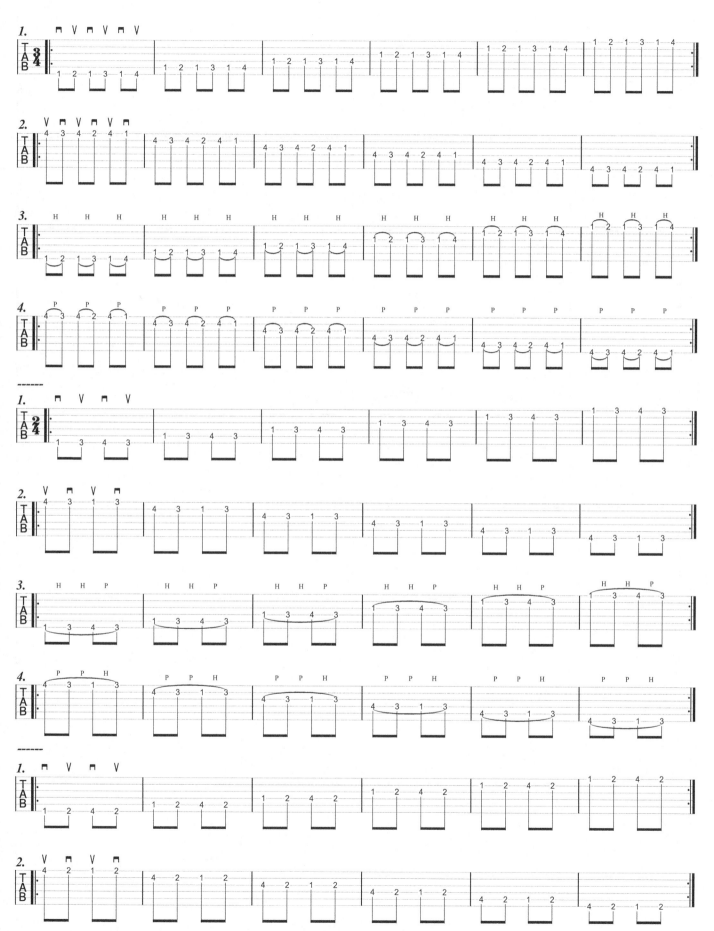

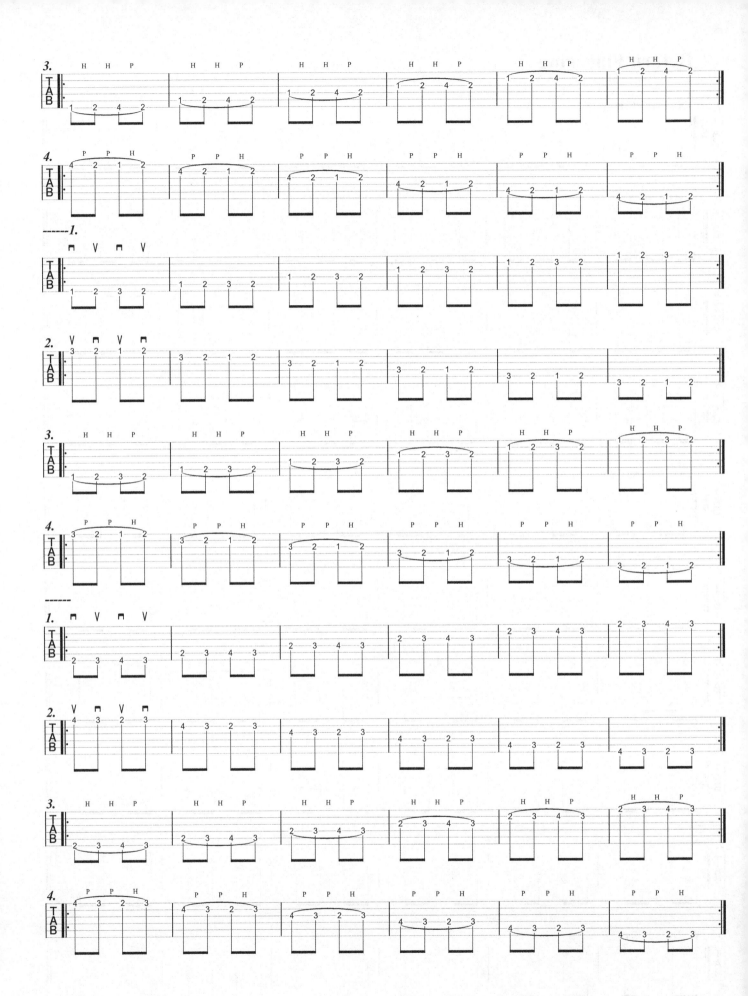

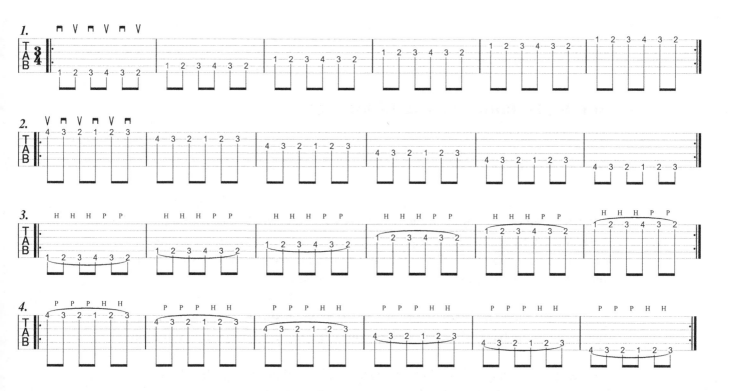

Sliding Hammer-ons and Pull-offs

When soloing or playing melodies, guitarists will employ legato techniques. These techniques include slides, hammer-ons, and pull-offs, and allow for smooth transitions between notes. These techniques can be applied to scales and melodies, making them sound smooth, connected, and stylistic.

Keep your fingers, including your thumb, light when shifting position. Move your thumb along the back of the neck with your hand to avoid dragging your thumb.

Follow the fingering below each exercise carefully. The straight line between the fret numbers, or sl., above the fret numbers indicates slide.

Recommended picking is shown in examples where necessary. Examples without picking patterns can be picked all down, all up, alternate, or a mix. The pick is only needed to set the string in motion while the hammer-ons, pull-offs, or slides keep the sound going.

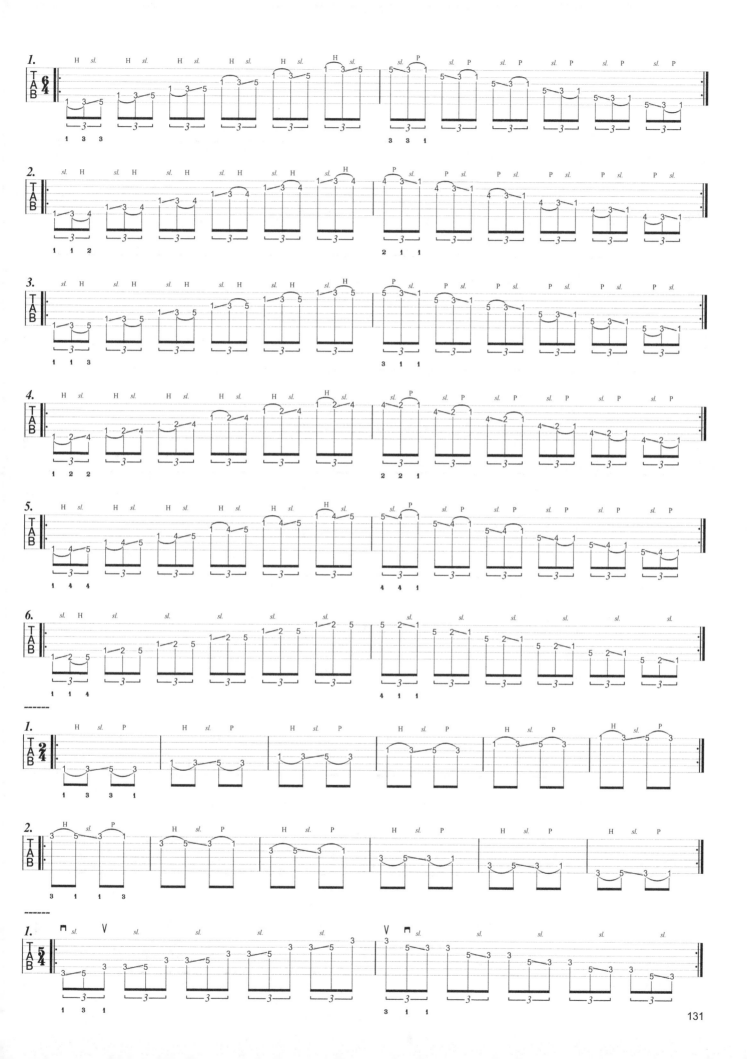

131

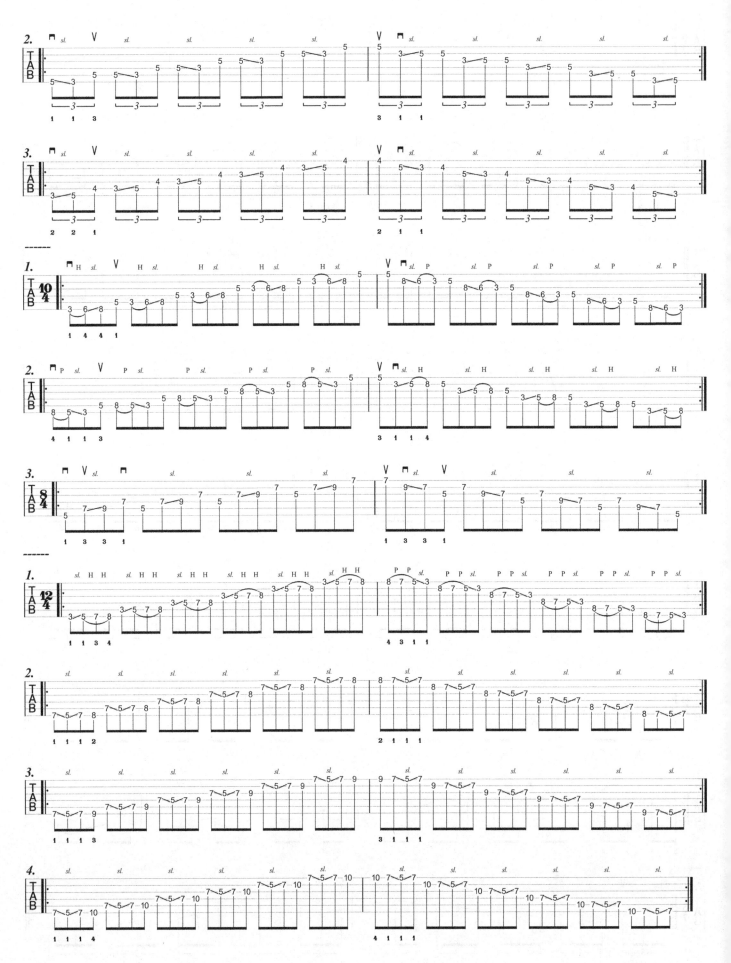

132

Spider Walks

Considered by many guitarists to be fun exercises, spider walks are a type of walking across the strings where your hand moves like a spider. There are basically two types of exercises that are considered spider walks: 1. A finger pattern that progresses from one string to the next. 2. One note per string is played in the manner of an arpeggio.

These are great for string crossing for both alternate picking and economy picking.

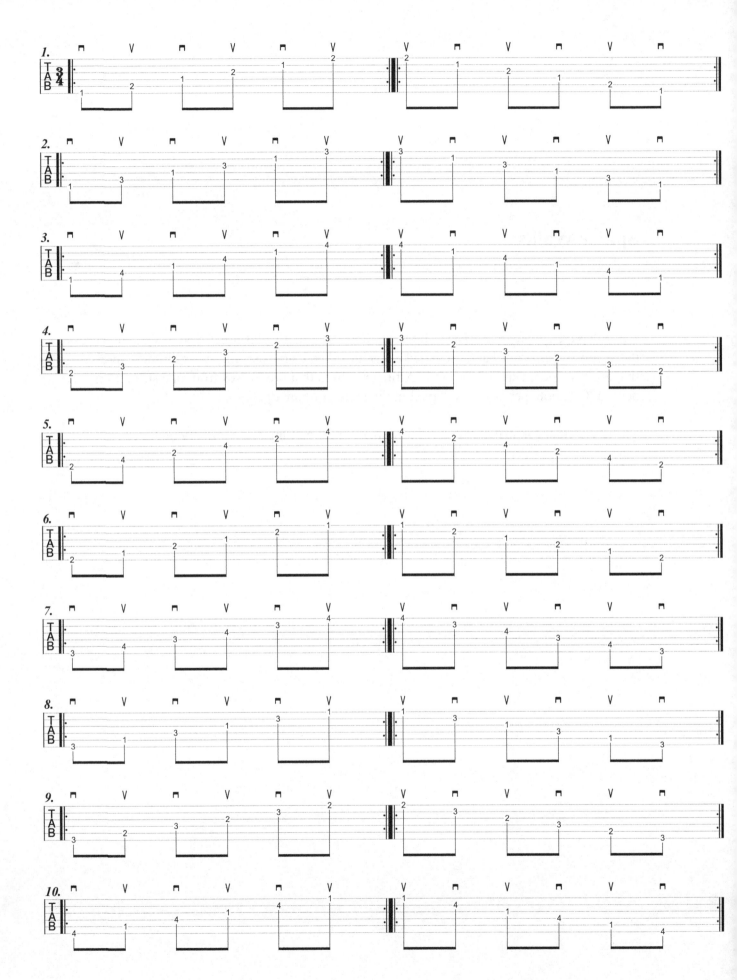

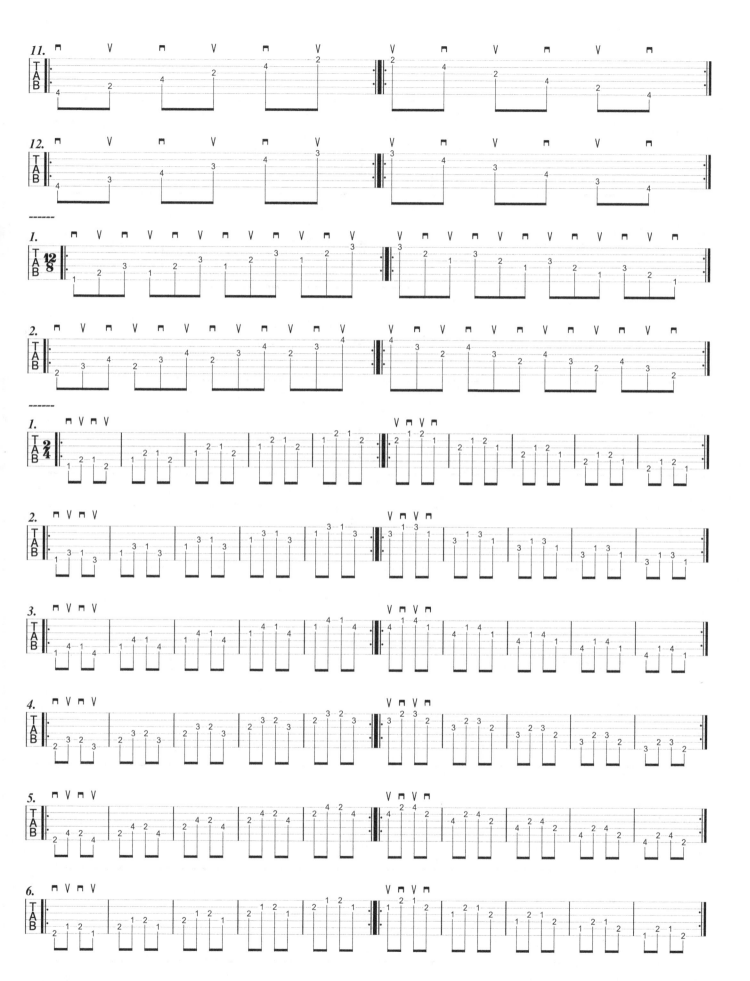

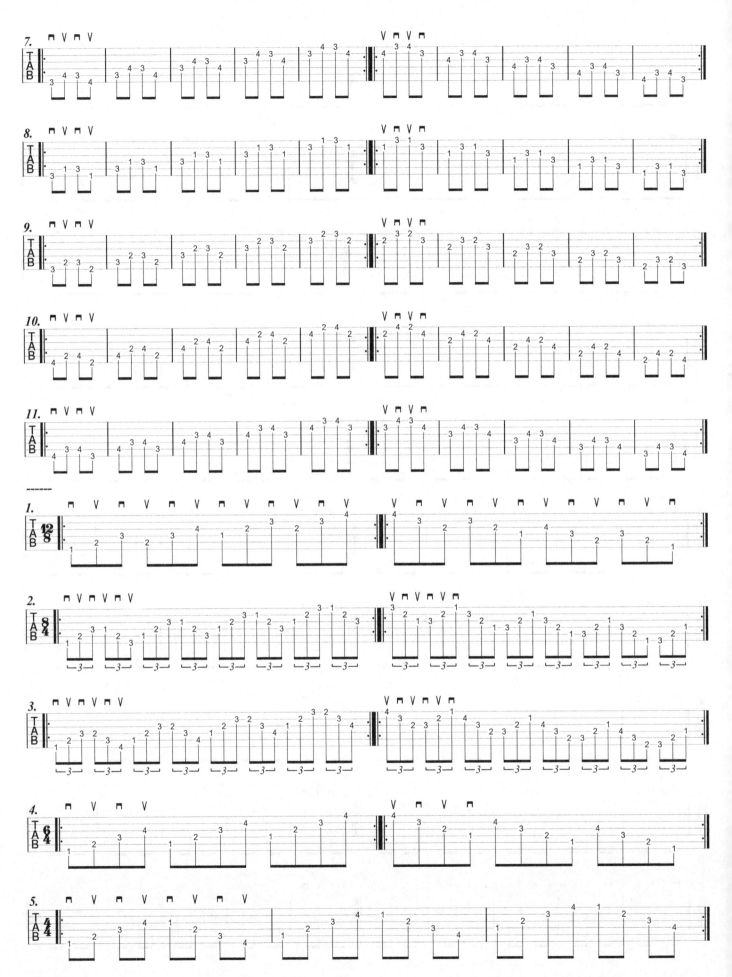

136

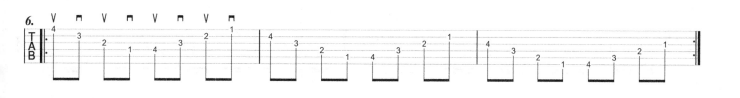

Spider Walks 2

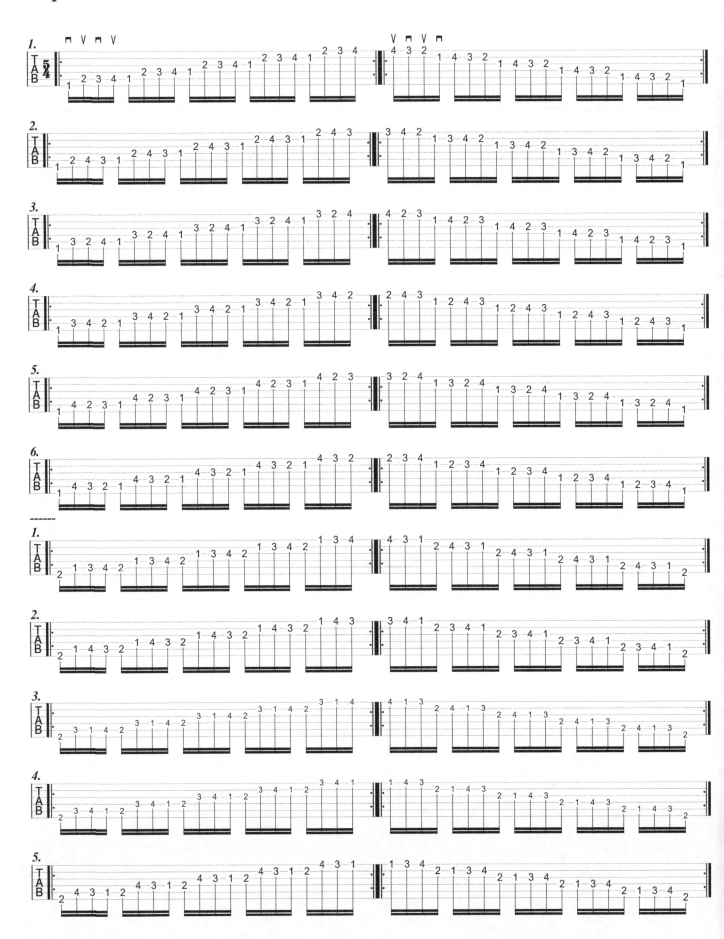

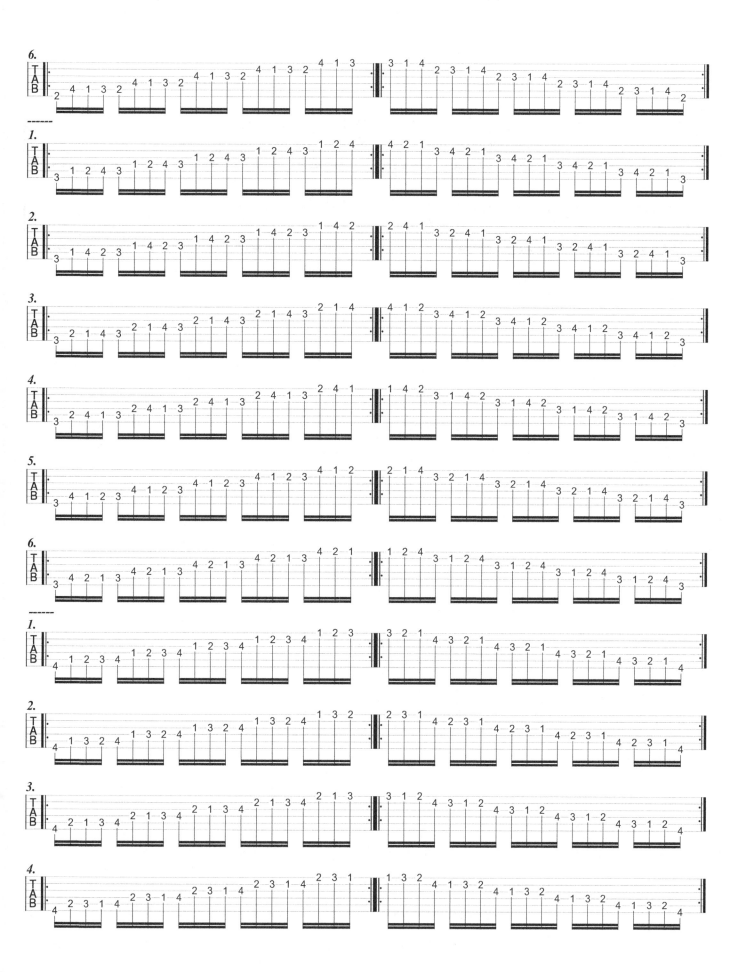

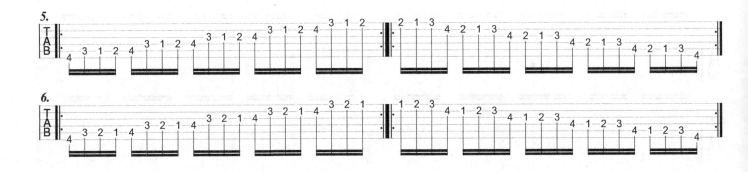

Spider Walks 3

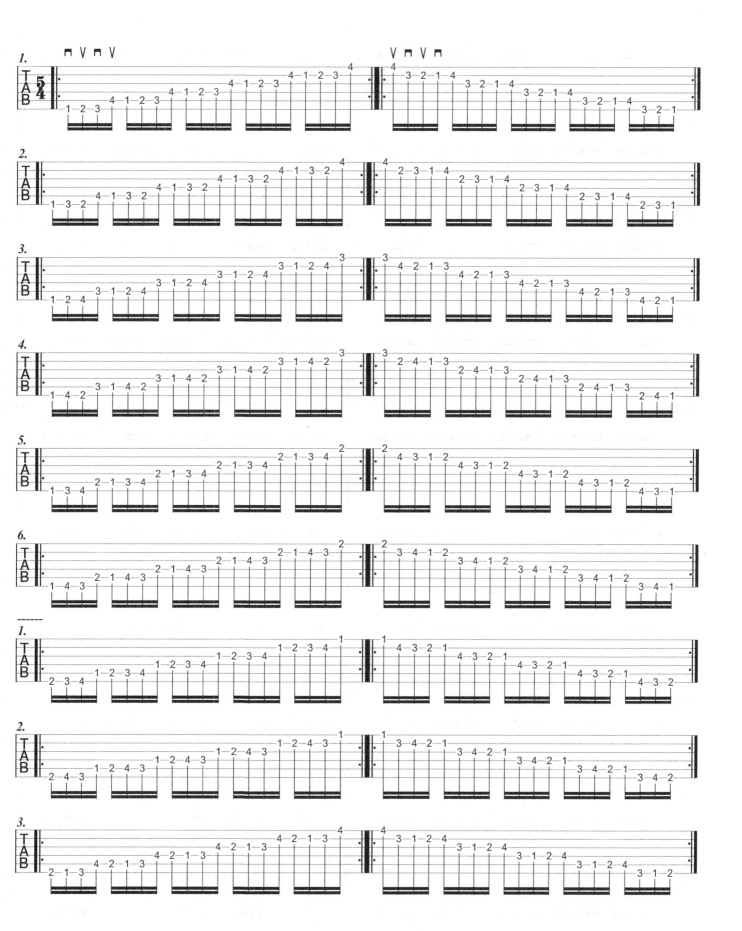

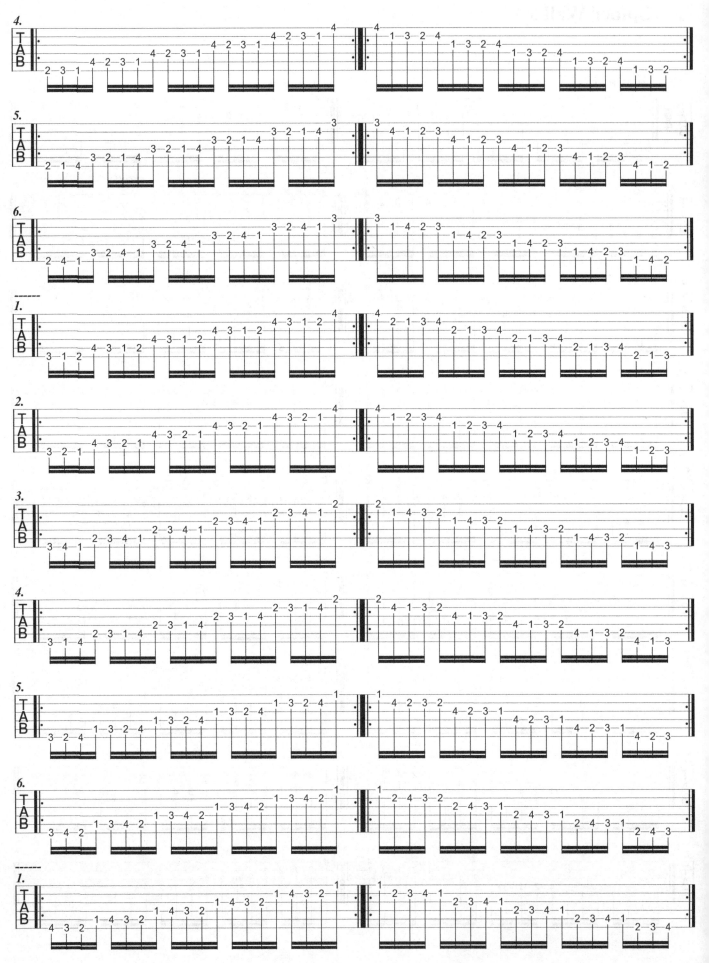

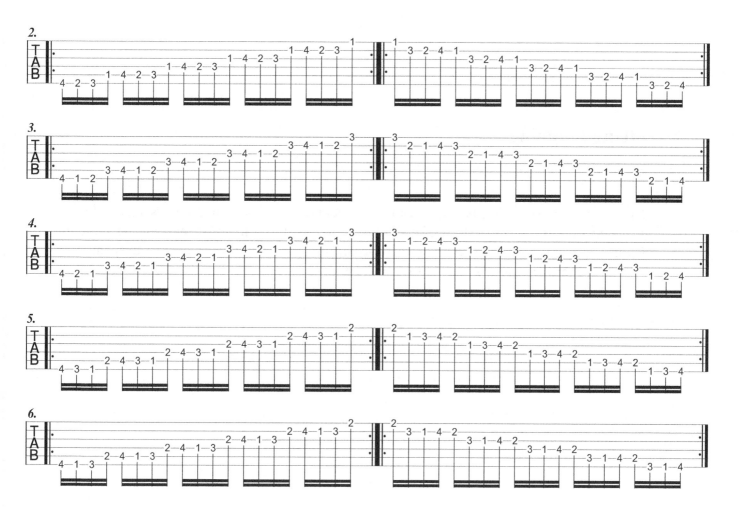

String Skipping

When skipping strings, it is best to use alternate picking. This is because there is a natural arc that occurs when you skip a string that allows you to miss the string or strings you are skipping. String skipping is mainly an accuracy exercise because you have to jump over strings, and as with most exercises, there is a benefit for both hands.

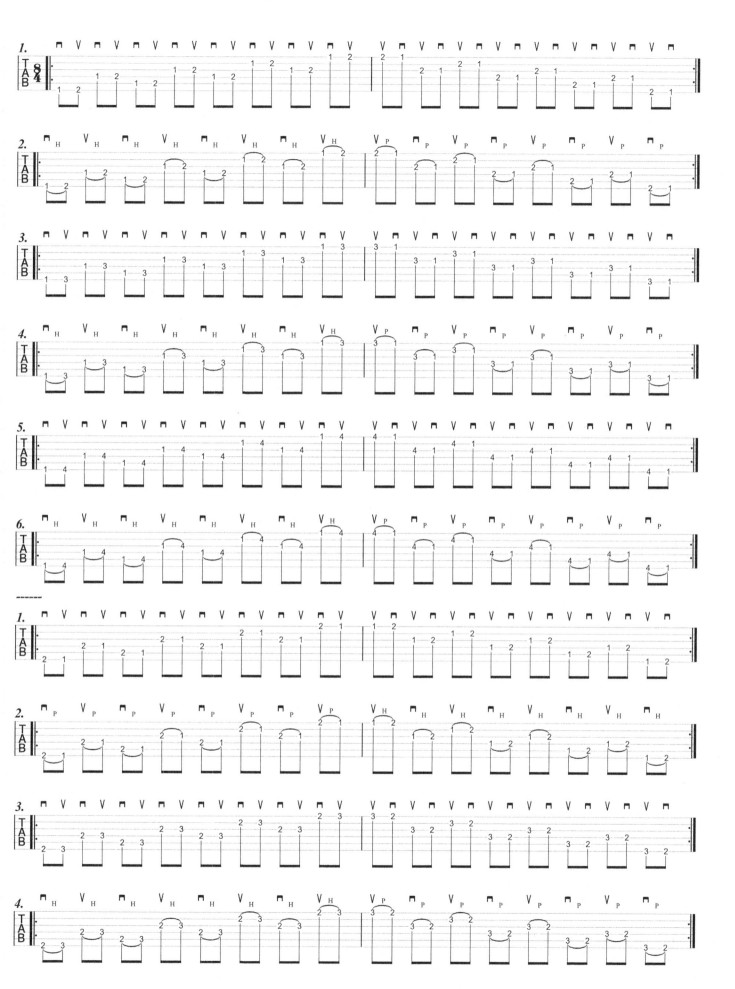

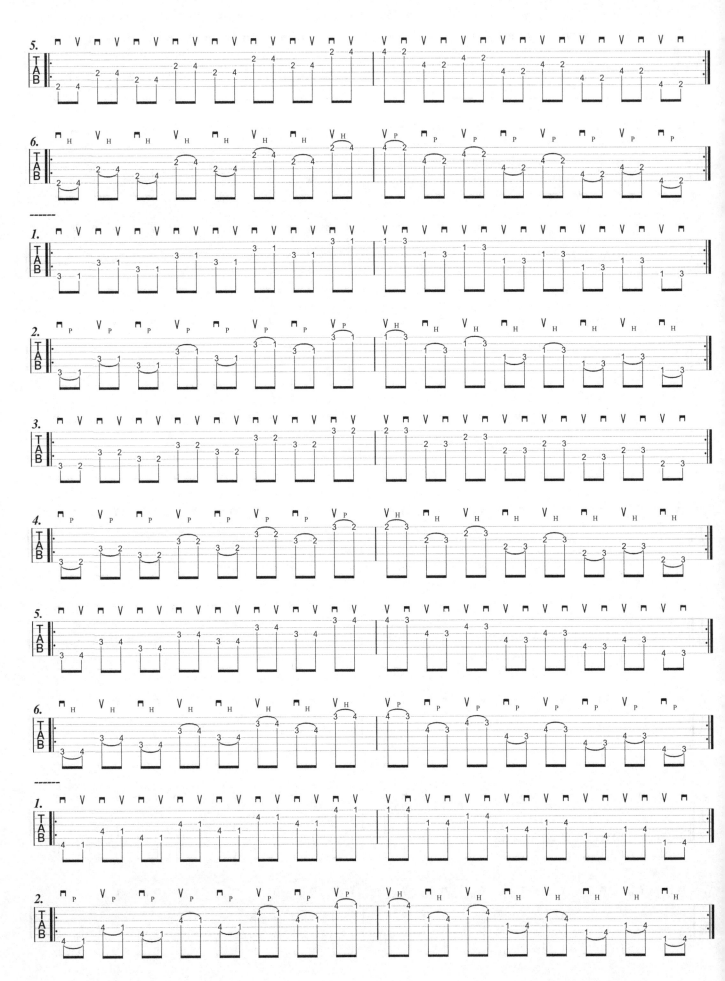

146

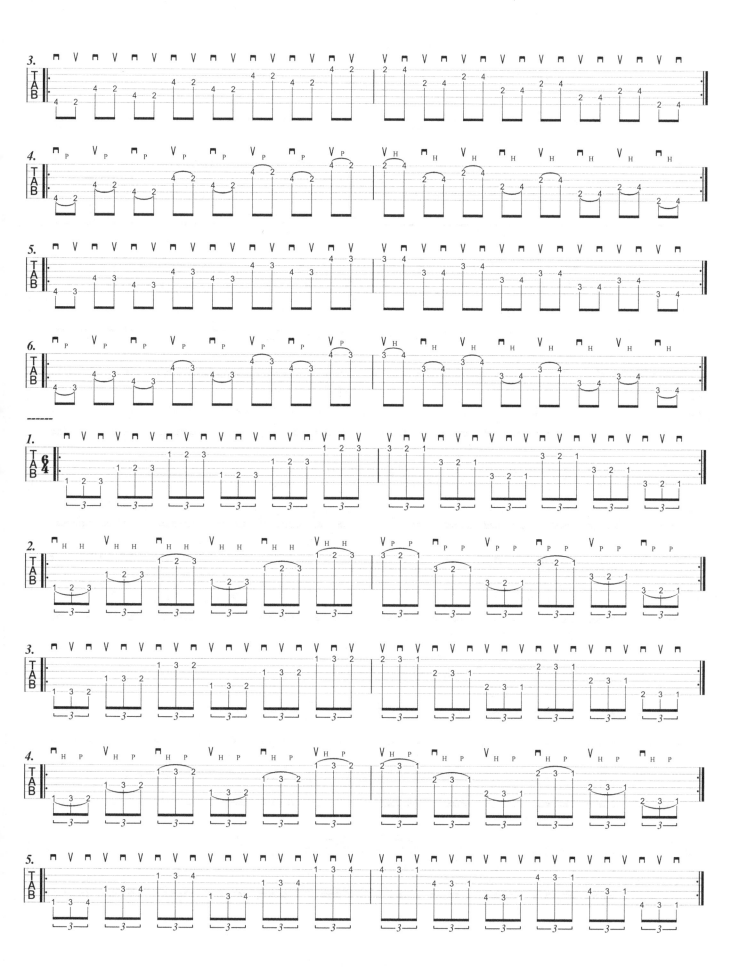

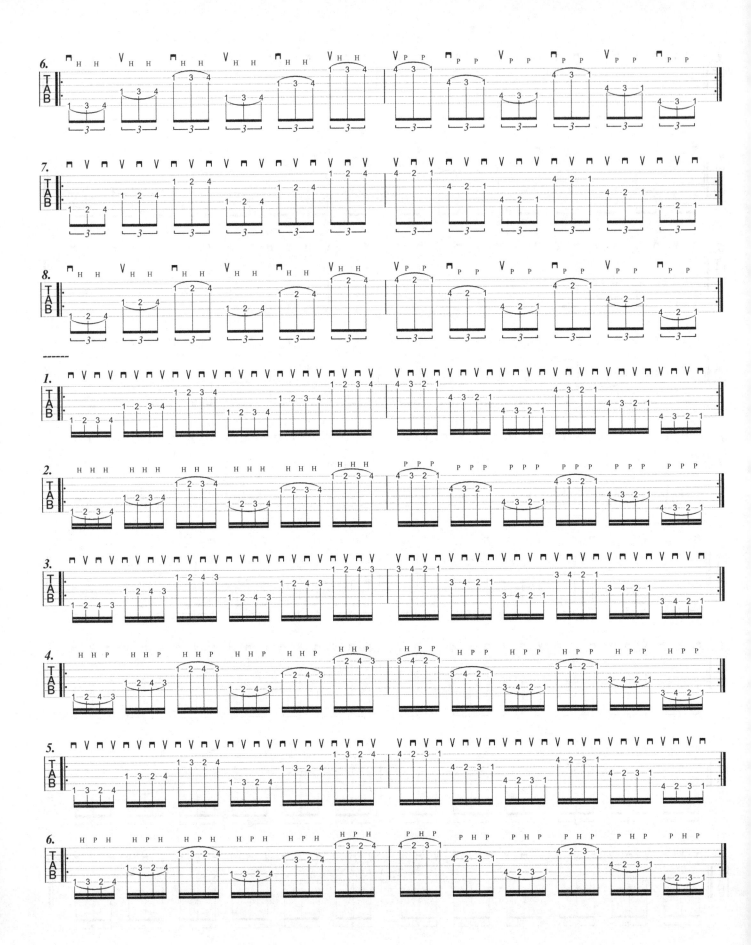

148

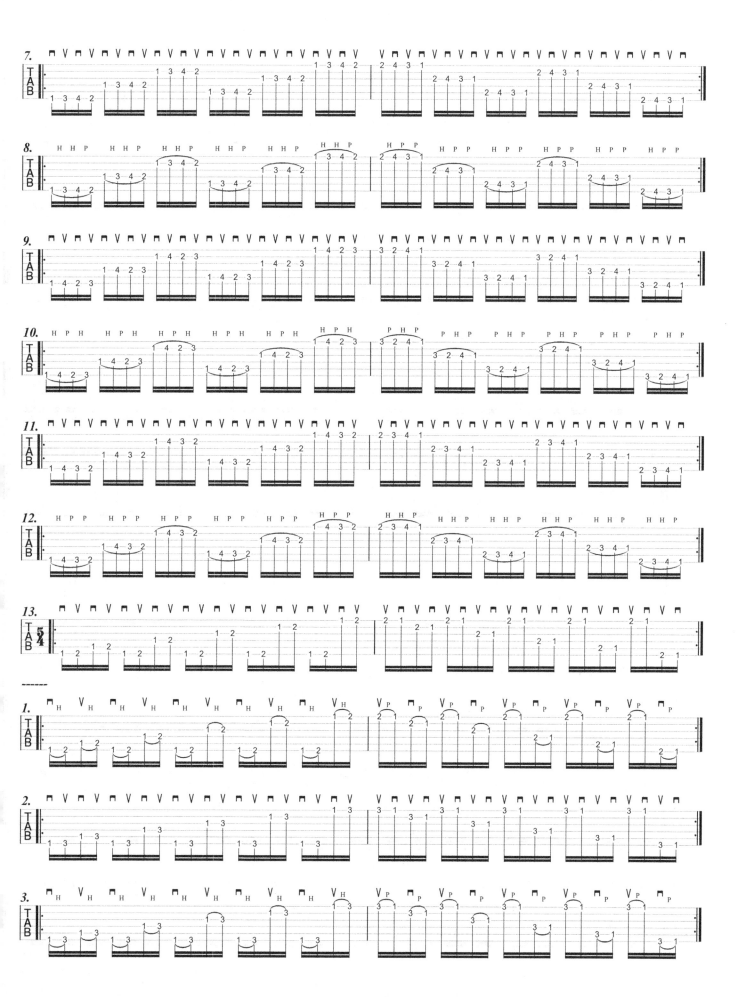

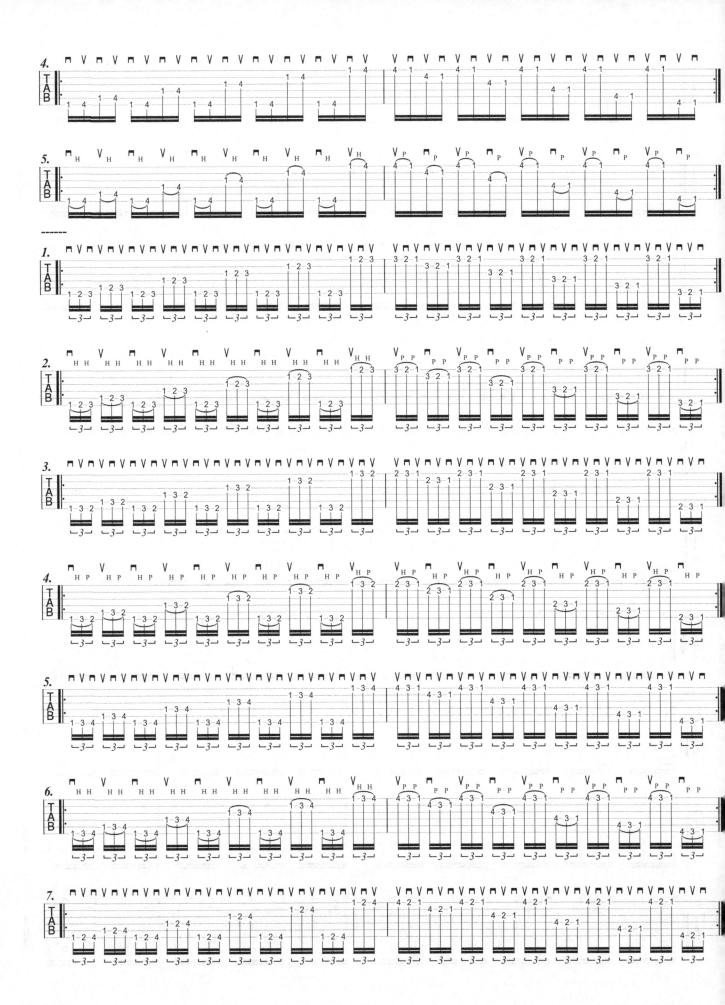

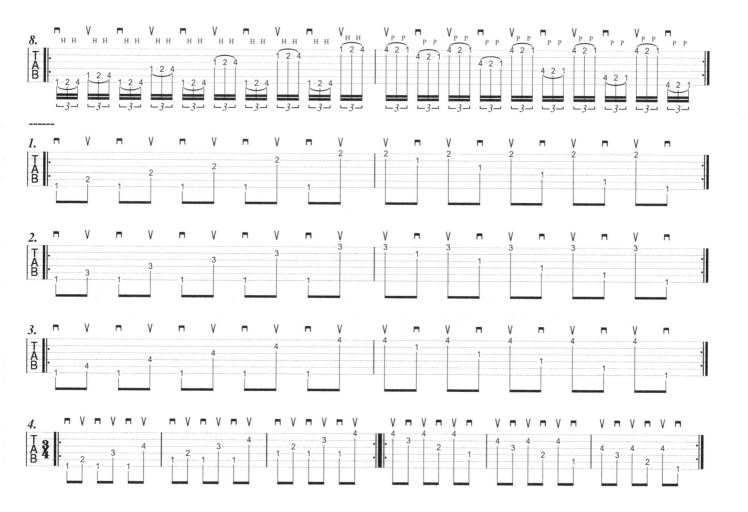

Sweeping

Sweep picking and economy picking are basically the same thing, but many guitarists think of sweeping in relation to arpeggios. Sweeping is achieved by brushing over the strings one note at a time, in the same direction, much like a strum. When strumming, the fingers stay on the strings. With arpeggios, the fingers lift after each note is played. The following exercises should be played like arpeggios.

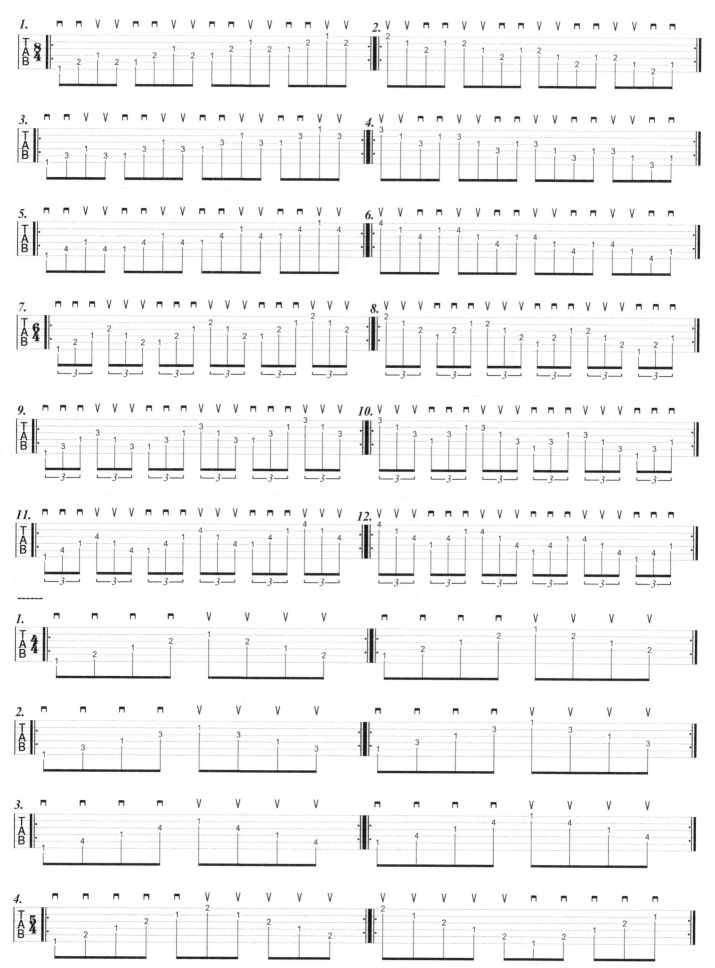

153

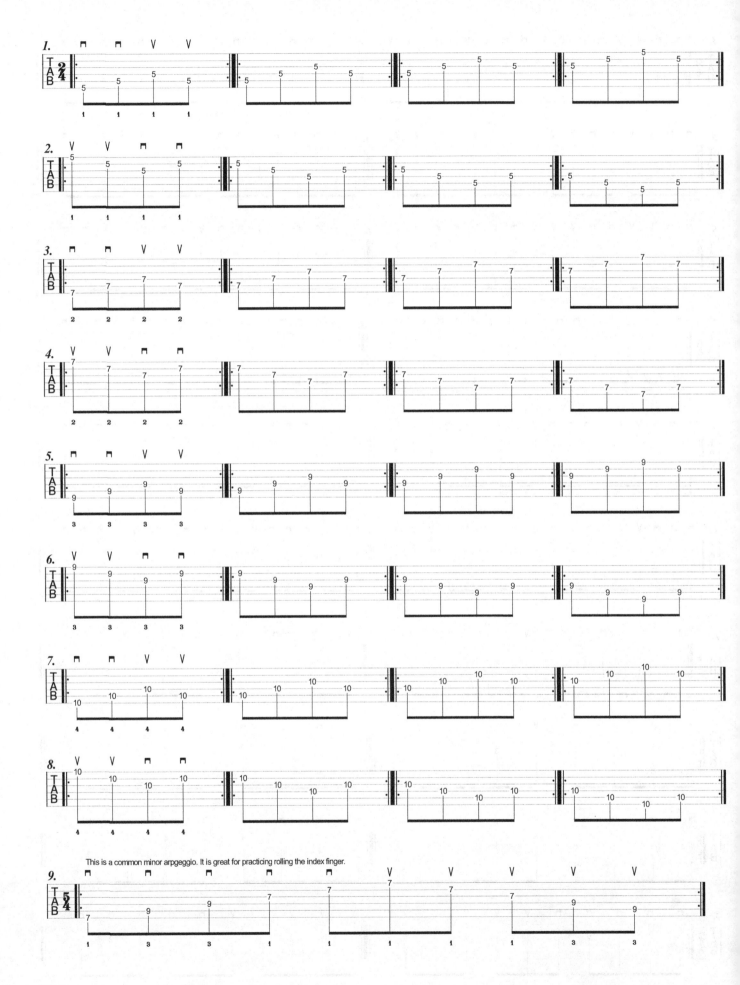

This is a common minor arpeggio. It is great for practicing rolling the index finger.

Tapping

Tapping can be performed with the index, middle, or any finger or combination of fingers on either hand! We will be focusing on using your index or middle fingers. If you use your index finger, you will have to either put your pick down or *palm* the pick by sliding it down and into your palm. If you use your middle finger, the pick can stay as usual between your index finger and thumb.

Tapping isn't really a tap but more like a press, like a hammer-on or pull-off. Stay as close to the fretbar as possible. For example, when tapping from a higher fret and releasing to a lower fret, you press the tap like a hammer-on and then do a slight pull-off to set the string in motion.

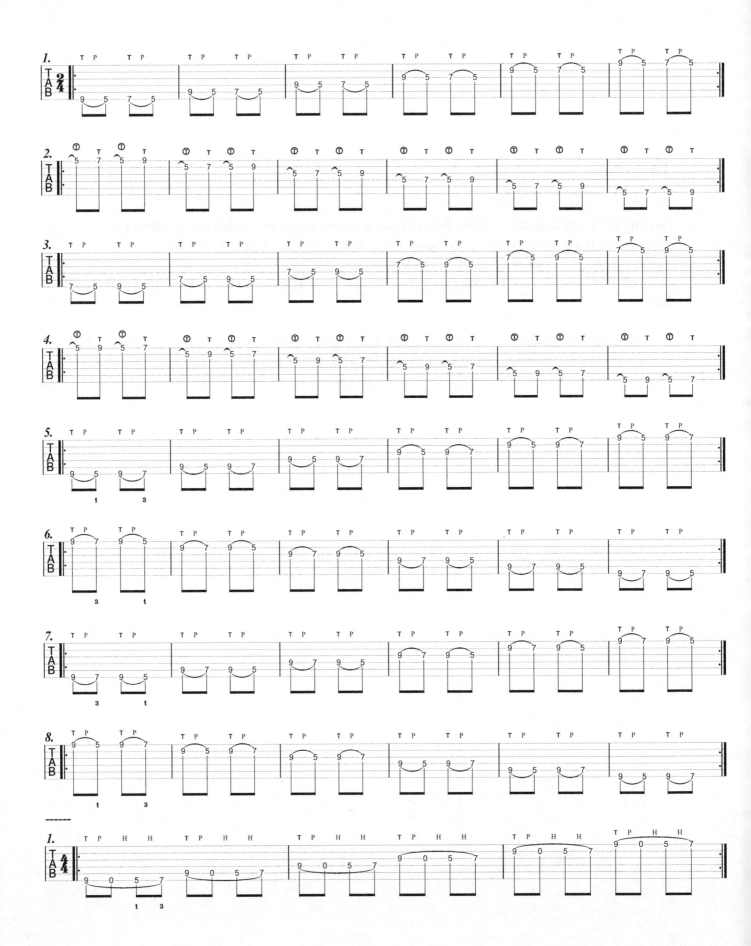

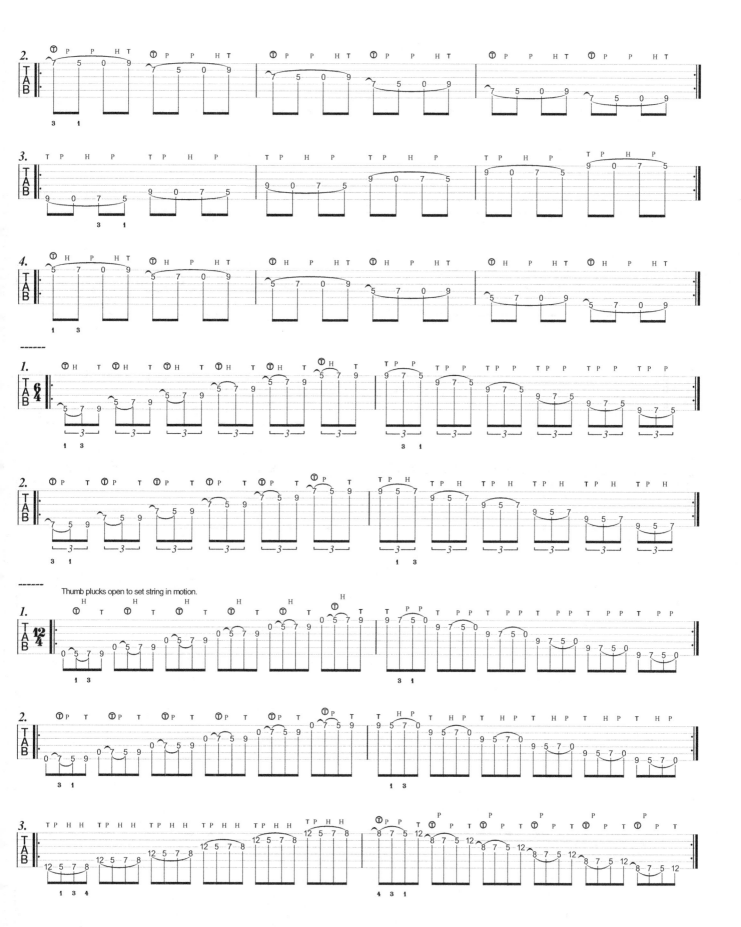

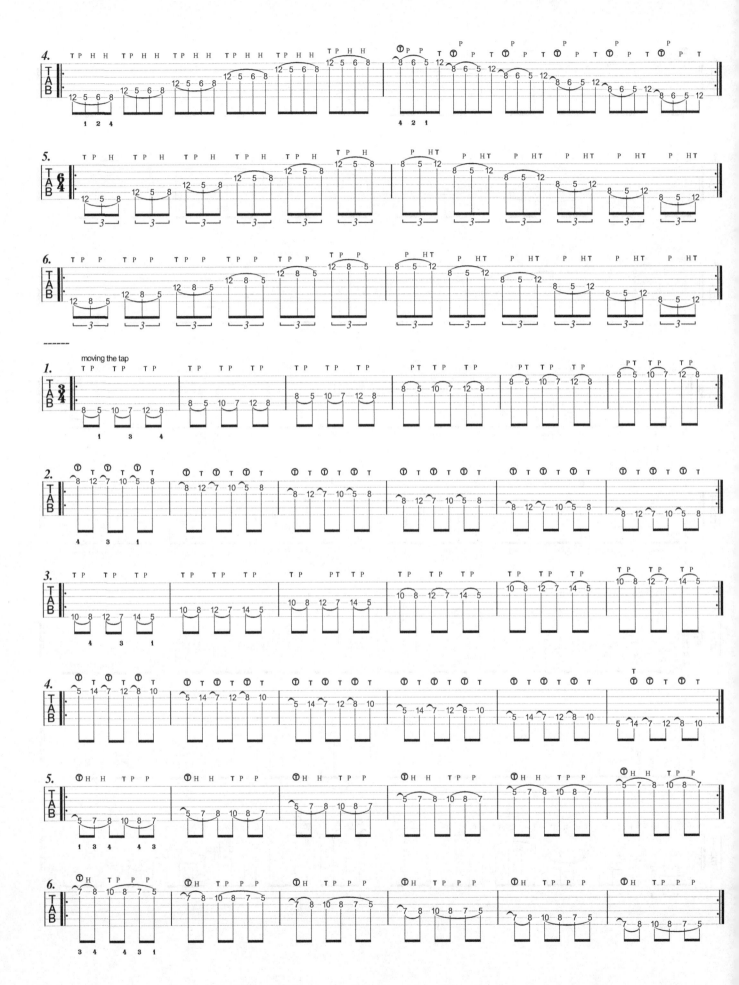

158

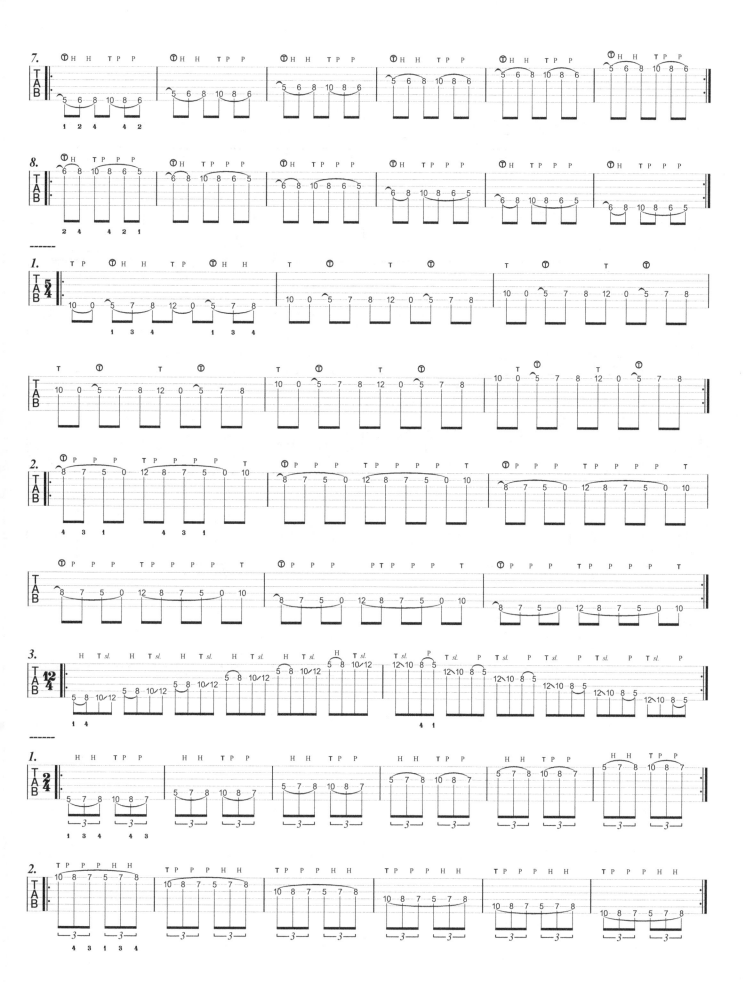

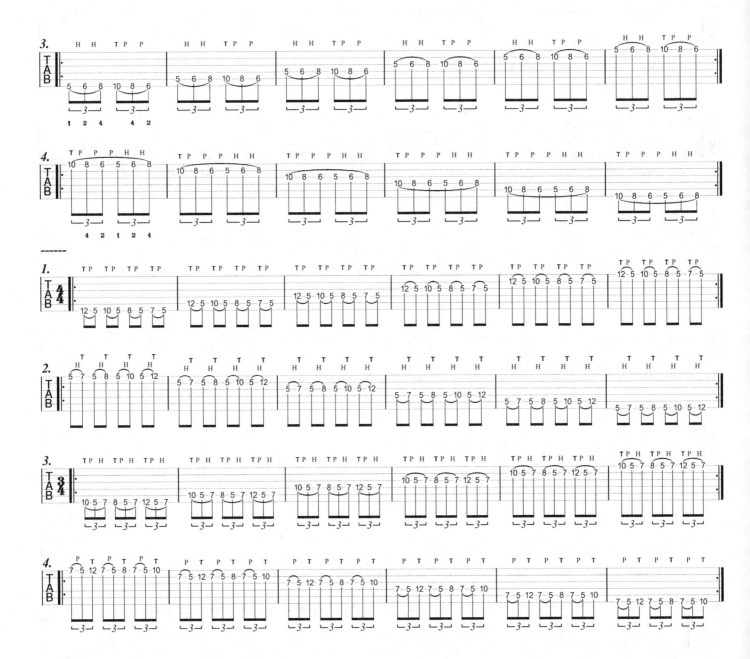

Two Handed Tapping

These two-handed tapping exercises require all four fingers of both hands to be used. The tapping technique is the same as tapping with a single finger; treat the pick hand fingers much like the fretting hand, where the *tapping* is performed similarly to hammer-ons and pull-offs from the fretting hand. These exercises are not for all guitarists, but two-handed tapping is becoming popular in the guitar world. Many two-handed tappers only use their index and middle fingers of their picking hand for tapping.

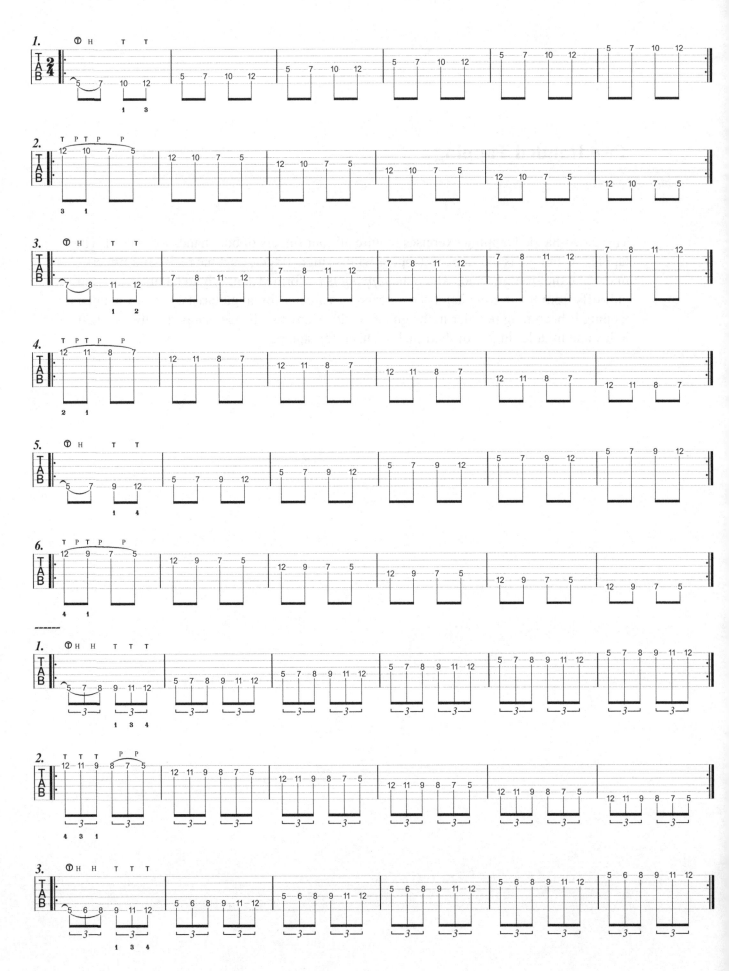

162

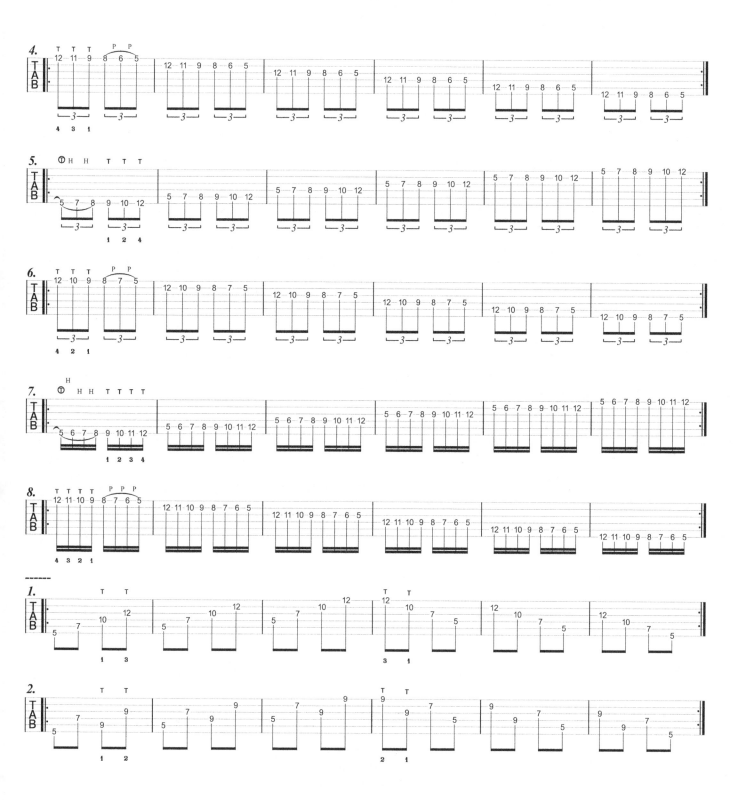

Thank you for your support!

For more books and materials, visit:

www.allaboutguitarbooks.com

Made in the USA
Monee, IL
25 September 2024

66547553R00090